The Hillary Effect

The Hillary Effect

Perspectives on Clinton's Legacy

Ivy A. M. Cargile, Denise S. Davis, Jennifer L. Merolla,
and Rachel VanSickle-Ward

I.B. TAURIS

LONDON • NEW YORK • OXFORD • NEW DELHI • SYDNEY

I.B. TAURIS

Bloomsbury Publishing Plc

50 Bedford Square, London, WC1B 3DP, UK

1385 Broadway, New York, NY 10018, USA

BLOOMSBURY, I.B. TAURIS and the I.B. Tauris logo are trademarks
of Bloomsbury Publishing Plc

First published in Great Britain 2020

Cover design by Adriana Brioso
Cover background © cienpies/Getty Images

A catalogue record for this book is available from the British Library.

A catalogue record for this book is available from the Library of Congress.

ISBN: HB: 978-1-8386-0393-9
      PB: 978-1-8386-0392-2
      ePDF: 978-1-8386-0394-6
      eBook: 978-1-8386-0395-3

Typeset by Deanta Global Publishing Services, Chennai, India

To find out more about our authors and books visit www.bloomsbury.com and
sign up for our newsletters.

For our families, and for Hillary.

Contents

Acknowledgments   x

About the Contributors   xi

Prologue: The Path up Is Always a Jagged Line *Gloria Steinem*   xxvi

Introduction *Jennifer L. Merolla and Rachel VanSickle-Ward*   1

Part One "I'm With Her": Clinton's Impact on Women's Lives
    and Ambitions

Preface *Jennifer L. Merolla*   9

  1 The Stories Not Told: Misrepresenting the Women Who Loved
      Clinton *Jennifer M. Piscopo*   13

  2 Parallel Lives *Debra Van Sickle*   17

  3 Listening Her Way to a Historic Victory: On Hillary Clinton's
      1999–2000 Senate Campaign *Kathleen A. Feeley*   20

  4 Recognition *Jennifer Chudy*   24

  5 Clarity in the Chaos: A New (and Improved) Vision of
      Motherhood, Faith, and Feminism *Jaclyn Cohen*   27

  6 From Fraud to Fighter *Brinda Sarathy*   31

Part Two "Agents of Change, Drivers of Progress" Clinton's Role
    in Shaping Activism

Preface *Denise S. Davis*   37

  7 Clinton Does Inspire: The Narrative About Hillary Clinton's
      "Enthusiasm Gap" Silences the Political Voices of Women
      Rachel VanSickle-Ward and Jennifer L. Merolla   40

  8 Dolores Speaks: Hillary's Influence on Activism and Politics
      Dolores Huerta and Ivy A. M. Cargile   43

  9 My Personal Hillary Effect *Torie Osborn*   47

 10 Pantsuit Nation *Jenn Carson*   50

 11 Glass Tumblers *Dc Lozano*   53

 12 Failure Is Impossible *Paulette Brown-Hinds*   56

 13 The #Resistance Tips Its Pussy Hat to HRC *Casey B. K. Dominguez*   59

14 The Hillary (Counterfactual) Effect: A Peculiar Paradox of Policy
    History and the Influence of Black Political Activism
    Shayla C. Nunnally   62

Part Three "When There Are No Ceilings, the Sky's the Limit":
    Clinton's Impact on Campaigns and Elections

Preface *Ivy A. M. Cargile*   71
15 Hillary Clinton: The Exception and the Rule *Carrie Skulley*   76
16 Battling Stereotypes of Women as Weak on National Security
    Mirya R. Holman, Jennifer L. Merolla, and Elizabeth J. Zechmeister   81
17 Rethinking Gender as an Electoral Asset *Kelly Dittmar*   86
18 A Mother for President: Motherhood Takes Center Stage at the
    DNC *Rachel VanSickle-Ward and Jill S. Greenlee*   89
19 Turing Point: Hillary Clinton's Impact on Latino Politics
    Adrian D. Pantoja   92
20 Latinas and Clinton's 2016 Campaign *Christina Bejarano*   96
21 Not in "Mixed Company"?: Courageous Conversations About
    Women and the Race Gap in American Politics *Lorrie Frasure*   99
22 The Year After *A'shanti F. Gholar*   104
23 Running because of Hillary *Denise S. Davis*   107
24 Stronger Together: How Hillary Clinton May Have Nudged
    More Women to Run for Office *Kristin Kanthak*   110

Part Four "Our Children Are Watching": Clinton's Impact on
    Parents and Kids

Preface *Jennifer L. Merolla*   115
25 Even in Defeat, Clinton's Campaign Could Still Inspire
    Young Women *Christina Wolbrecht and David Campbell*   119
26 Hillary Clinton, My Daughter, and Me *Abby K. Wood*   122
27 Drawing Madam President: How Children Imagine Hillary
    Clinton as a Political Leader *Jill S. Greenlee, Angela L. Bos,*
    Mirya R. Holman, J. Celeste Lay, and Zoe M. Oxley   125
28 Real Moms of Palo Alto, Real Takeaways from Hillary's
    Candidacy *Melissa R. Michelson*   128
29 Fatherhood, First Daughters, and the First Woman Presidential
    Candidate *Elizabeth A. Sharrow, Jesse H. Rhodes, Tatishe M. Nteta,*
    and Jill S. Greenlee   131

Part Five "Deal Me in": Clinton's Impact on Policy

Preface *Rachel VanSickle-Ward*   137
30 Standing Her Ground on Foreign Policy *Roselyn Hsueh*   141
31 "Women's Rights Are Human Rights" *Celeste Montoya*   145
32 Global Gender Effects: The Impact of Hillary Clinton on
     American Foreign Policy *Sara Angevine*   149
33 The Backbone of Democracy: Clinton, Women of Color
     and the Fight for Voting Rights *Ivy A. M. Cargile*   154
34 The "Economic Woman": Why Clinton's Economic Message
     Still Matters *Rachel VanSickle-Ward and Emma Stephens*   158
35 The Wisdom of a Wonky Woman: Reflecting on Clinton's Approach
     to Policy on the Campaign Trail *Rachel VanSickle-Ward*   162

Conclusion *Jennifer L. Merolla and Rachel VanSickle-Ward*   166

Notes   169
Index   178

Acknowledgments

This book is a work of collaboration, and we are deeply grateful to everyone who made it possible. First and foremost, thank you to the wonderful contributors. The chapters are short, but the work and thought behind them is considerable. Often they represent years of research and/or professional efforts. In some cases they include discussion of deeply personal experiences. We are grateful to our contributors for their brilliant pieces, and for the trust they put in us as editors to put the pieces together.

We are further grateful to colleagues who offered guidance and support as we developed this project. Many of these folks are contributors, others include Kim Dionne, Amanda Hollis-Brusky, Matt Grossman, Jane Junn, Laura Stephenson, John Sides, and Kathy Yep. Pitzer students in Professor VanSickle-Ward's Women in Politics senior seminar offered thoughtful feedback as well.

Our thanks also go to our editorial team at Bloomsbury Publishing. This volume would not be possible without the enthusiasm, support and guidance of Nayiri Kendir and Tomasz Hoskins. Leela Ulaganathan shepherded us through the production process with patience and care. Reviewers provided constructive commentary, and the volume is significantly improved by their recommendations. We are further grateful to institutional support provided by Pitzer College, California State University, Bakersfield, and the University of California, Riverside.

On a personal note, and especially because this book is a labor of love, we want to thank the many loved ones who supported us in the endeavor. Rachel would particularly like to thank Neil, her wonderful kids, Mom, Andy, Dad, Deb, Mitch, Zack, Joel, Carrie and Rich. Jennifer would like to thank Andy, her empathetic son, her spirited daughter, and her supportive parents and in-laws. Ivy would like to thank Brian for always being so steadfast in his support of all she does, her brilliant group of women friends who never leave her side, and her amazing mother who taught her to be ambitious, confident and strong. Denise would like to thank her mother, Suze, who introduced her to Hillary's work and impact at a young age and has always been her inspiration to do good in the world.

And, last but not least, we would like to thank Hillary Rodham Clinton, for her decades of public service and dedication to amplifying the voices of those who have traditionally not been given a seat at the table of politics.

About the Contributors

Sara Angevine is an assistant professor of Political Science at Whittier College in Whittier, California. Her research and teaching interests focus on women and politics. Currently, she is working on a book manuscript that examines the policy objectives of, and congressional motivations behind, women's rights in US foreign policy. Angevine received her PhD in Political Science at Rutgers University-New Brunswick in 2014. She earned a Master's in Women's and Gender Studies at the University of the Western Cape, Bellville, South Africa, and an International Gender Studies Certificate from Utrecht University in The Netherlands. She has advanced training in quantitative, qualitative and feminist research methods. Prior to Whittier, Angevine taught political science and gender studies courses at Brooklyn College, CUNY; Barnard College, Columbia University; and Rutgers University, New Brunswick. She also spent one year living in Ljubljana, Slovenia, teaching English. Before graduate school, she worked on federal election campaigns in the United States in Indiana (2002) and Oregon (2004). Originally from Madison, Wisconsin, she currently resides in Long Beach, California, where she enjoys playing beach volleyball, learning the nuances of California food culture and creating her own definition of seasons.

Christina Bejarano is Professor of Multicultural Women's and Gender Studies at Texas Woman's University. She received her bachelor's from the University of North Texas and her Master's and PhD from the University of Iowa. She is a nationally recognized author, speaker and adviser on Latina electoral politics in the United States. She studies the conditions under which racial/ethnic minorities and women successfully compete for US electoral office, which is reflected in her book on Latina political candidates, *The Latina Advantage: Gender, Race, and Political Success* (2013). Her work also focuses on how racial/ethnic minorities and women can shape or influence the current electoral environment, which is reflected in her second book, *The Latino Gender Gap in U.S. Politics* (2014).

Angela L. Bos is an associate professor of Political Science and associate dean of Experiential Learning at the College of Wooster. She received her Master's and PhD in American Politics and a PhD minor in Political Psychology in 2007 from the University of Minnesota and her Bachelor's in Political Science from the University of Minnesota-Morris. Bos studies and teaches courses about American Politics on topics such as women and politics, political psychology, civic education and media and politics. She coedited the book *The Political Psychology of Women in U.S. Politics* (2016) and has published in journals such as *Political Psychology, Political Communication, Politics & Gender,* and the *Journal of Applied Social Psychology.*

Dr. Paulette Brown-Hinds is the founder of Voice Media Ventures and the second-generation publisher of *The Black Voice News.* She is an award-winning columnist and Knight Digital Media Fellow, with nearly thirty years' experience in media, communications and community engagement. She is the president of the California News Publishers Association, the first African American to lead the organization in its 130-year history. She also sits on the boards of the Community Foundation of Inland Southern California, the California Press Foundation and the James Irvine Foundation.

She earned a Bachelor's in English Literature from CSU San Bernardino and her Master's and PhD from UC Riverside in English Literature. She leads Underground Railroad Study Tours for the Black Voice Foundation, stewards a collection of rare antebellum slavery artifacts and teaches a course at UCR on arts, enterprise and the community. Brown-Hinds is the founder of Mapping Black California, a geospatial technology community mapping GIS and STEAM initiative, with a goal of building a "smart and connected" African American community in the Golden State.

David Campbell is the Packey J. Dee Professor of American Democracy at the University of Notre Dame and the chairperson of the Political Science Department. His most recent book is *Seeking the Promised Land: Mormons and American Politics* (with John Green and Quin Monson). He is also the co-author (with Robert Putnam) of *American Grace: How Religion Divides and Unites Us,* which has been described by the *New York Times* as intellectually powerful; by *America* as an instant classic; and by the *San Francisco Chronicle* as the most successfully argued sociological study of American religion in more than half a century. *American Grace* has also received both the 2011 Woodrow Wilson Award from the American Political Science Association for the best book on government, politics or international affairs and the Wilbur Award from the Religious Communicators Council for the best non-fiction book of 2010.

Campbell is also the author of *Why We Vote: How Schools and Communities Shape Our Civic Life,* the editor of *A Matter of Faith: Religion in the 2004 Presidential Election* and a co-editor of *Making Civics Count: Citizenship*

Education for a New Generation. As an expert on religion, politics and civic engagement, he has often been featured in the national media, including the *New York Times, Economist, USA Today, Washington Post, Wall Street Journal, Time*, NBC News, CNN, NPR, Fox News, and C-SPAN.

Ivy A.M. Cargile is an assistant professor of Political Science at California State University, Bakersfield. She received her bachelor's from California State University, Fullerton, and her Master's and PhD from Claremont Graduate University. Broadly, her research interests focus on political behavior in the US context. She is particularly interested in how the intersections of gender, race and ethnicity affect the electoral behavior of both political elites and the electorate at large. Specifically, she is interested in how diverse political participants perceive a Latina candidate who represents the intersection of gender and ethnicity. Likewise, she explores how both Latina political actors and other female politicians of color influence policy outcomes and represent their constituents. She also focuses some of her research on the public opinion of Latina/o/x voters as a way to develop a better understanding about how policy issues, such as immigration and women's rights, affect the participation of this community. Her work has appeared in *Political Research Quarterly, Urban Affairs Review* as well as in multiple books on the topics of Latina politicians, Latin@/x voters and immigration policy.

Jenn Carson is an advocate for children of prisoners and violent crime victims. She is also a public advocate for mental health. She received her bachelor's in History from Baylor University and her Master's in Counseling from George Washington University. She is an alumna of Teach For America with fifteen years' experience as a public educator. On the Hallmark Channel, the Oxygen Network, the Today Show, BBC Radio and in *Marie Claire* Magazine and *Huffington Post*, she has shared her journey from a nine-year-old suicidal daughter of a convicted murderer to an advocate. As a plus size woman with PTSD, as sexual assault survivor and as the child of a prisoner, Jenn has also written and spoken extensively on violence against women, parental incarceration and body positivity. Jenn is a board member of Women's March California and the leader of Pantsuit Nation Inland Empire. She is also an ex-Republican who proudly wore a shabby dated pantsuit to the polls to vote for Hillary Clinton in 2016.

Jennifer Chudy is an assistant professor of Political Science at Wellesley College. She received her bachelor's from Brown University and her Master's and PhD from the University of Michigan. Her research focuses on the influence of racial attitudes in public opinion. Specifically, her dissertation argues that racial sympathy—defined as white distress over black suffering—plays an influential role in American politics. She has published her work in *The Forum* and the *Journal of Politics*. Her first entry into politics was as an intern in Senator Hillary Rodham Clinton's New York City office from 2003–5. Subsequently, she worked for the New York City Department of Homeless Services, Mayor Bloomberg and the Clinton Global Initiative before pursuing a career in academia.

Jaclyn Cohen is a rabbi, writer, musician, yoga teacher, wife, mother and maternal and mental health advocate based in Los Angeles. She was ordained in 2014 by the Hebrew Union College-Jewish Institute of Religion, and currently serves Temple Isaiah in West Los Angeles. She has authored several articles and delivered presentations on the topics of women's health, spiritual wellness, faith and feminism and mental health. She serves as a volunteer and speaker for Maternal Mental Health Now as well as for the Jewish Center for Justice and Planned Parenthood.

Denise S. Davis is the director of the Women's Resource Center at the University of California, Riverside. She received her bachelor's from the University of Redlands and her Master's from the London School of Economics. Denise has spent her career working in student affairs and teaching gender and sexuality studies in higher education. She is passionate about issues pertaining to social justice advocacy, gender equity, the LGBTQ community and women's political participation. In 2017, she launched the inaugural Persist Women's Political Engagement Conference at the University of California, Riverside, which was the first of its kind in the region. Denise is a graduate of the Emerge California program, and was elected to the Redlands City Council in 2018. Her election made history, as she is the first openly LGBTQ Council Member in the City of Redlands. She currently serves as Mayor Pro Tem.

Kelly Dittmar is an assistant professor of Political Science at Rutgers University-Camden and Scholar at the Center for American Women and Politics (CAWP) at the Eagleton Institute of Politics. She is the author of *Navigating Gendered Terrain: Stereotypes and Strategy in Political Campaigns* (2015), and co-author (with Kira Sanbonmatsu and Susan J. Carroll) of *A Seat at the Table: Congresswomen's Perspectives on Why Their Presence Matters* (2018). Dittmar's research focuses on gender and American political institutions. At CAWP, Dittmar manages national research projects, helps to develop and implement CAWP's research agenda and contributes to CAWP reports, publications and analyses. Dittmar was an

American Political Science Association (APSA) Congressional Fellow from 2011 to 2012 and is frequently an expert source and commentator for media outlets including MSNBC, NPR, PBS, the *New York Times* and the *Washington Post*. Dittmar earned her bachelor's from Aquinas College in Grand Rapids, Michigan and her PhD from Rutgers University-New Brunswick.

Casey B. K. Dominguez is Professor of Political Science and International Relations at the University of San Diego. She received her PhD in political science from UC Berkeley in 2005. Her research investigates the relationships among interest groups and political parties and the development of the US presidency.

Kathleen A. Feeley is Professor of History at University of Redlands. She is a co-coordinator of the Los Angeles History & Metro Studies Group of the Huntington-USC Institute on California and the West. Her teaching and research interests focus on media, gender and popular and political culture in modern America. She is co-editor of *When Private Talk Goes Public: Gossip in American History* (2014), author of *Mary Pickford: Hollywood and the New Woman* (2016), and is at work on *"The Mightiest Publicity Powers on Earth": The Hollywood Press Corps and the Making of the Modern Press in Mid-Twentieth-Century America*.

Lorrie Frasure is an associate professor of Political Science and African American Studies at the University of California-Los Angeles. Her research interests include racial/ethnic political behavior, immigrant political incorporation, African American politics, women and politics, and state and local politics. In 2015, she became the first woman of color to earn tenure and promotion in the Political Science Department at UCLA. Her book *Racial and Ethnic Politics in American Suburbs* is the 2016 winner of two national book awards by the American Political Science Association (APSA), including the Best Book about Race Relations in the United States from the Race, Ethnicity and Politics (REP) Section and the Dennis Judd Best Book Award in Urban and Local Politics. She was featured in the PBS Newshour "Rethinking College" segment highlighting her teaching and mentorship with first-generation college students at UCLA. Frasure was also featured in the UCLA First-Generation Faculty Initiative to encourage and inspire first-generation college students. She was awarded the University of Chicago's Harris School of Public Policy Rising Star Alumni Award for "extraordinary work addressing racial and ethnic politics in America."

She received her PhD and Master's in political science Political Science from the University of Maryland-College Park, a master's in Public Policy (MPP) from the University of Chicago, and a bachelor's in political science from the University of Illinois, Urbana-Champaign. Prior to joining the faculty of UCLA, she was a postdoctoral associate and visiting assistant professor in the Department of Government at Cornell University. She is a first-generation college graduate, born and raised on the Southside of Chicago.

A'shanti F. Gholar serves as the president of Emerge, the only organization dedicated to recruiting and training Democratic women to run for office. Gholar is a nationally recognized political strategist, who most recently served as Emerge's Political Director. She has experience in building coalitions, program development and community and political engagement. Prior to working with Emerge America, Gholar served as the National Deputy Director of Community Engagement and Director of African American Engagement for the Democratic National Committee. Gholar was recently named as one of She The People's 20 for 2020—a list of women of color in politics who will play an impactful role in the 2020 elections. She was featured as a political influencer in CQ Roll Call Magazine, named a top woman of color in policy by Walker's Legacy, and was awarded the "Changemaker" award by African American Women in Business Careers. Gholar is also the founder of The Brown Girls Guide to Politics, which was named one of the top podcasts to prepare people for the 2020 election by Marie Claire.

Jill S. Greenlee is an associate professor in Politics and Women's, Gender and Sexuality Studies at Brandeis University. She received her Bachelor's in Political Science from the University of Michigan and her PhD in Political Science from the University of California, Berkeley. She teaches courses in American politics and political behavior, focusing on topics connected to gender. Her scholarship engages with questions about political socialization both how individuals change politically over the life course and how political generations emerge. Her book *The Political Consequences of Motherhood* (2014) investigates the complex relationship between motherhood and female political attitudes, as well as explores how motherhood has been used in the American political landscape over time. She has continued to write about motherhood and fatherhood in several co-authored publications. Professor Greenlee has published work in journals such as *Political Psychology, Politics and Gender, Politics, Groups, and Identities, PS Political Science and Politics* and *Public Opinion Quarterly*.

Mirya R. Holman is Associate Professor of Political Science at Tulane University. She studies and teaches women and politics, urban politics and research methods. Her book *Women and Politics in the American City* focuses on the influence of gender on the behavior of mayors and city council members in the United States. She has published journal articles and book chapters in journals such as *Political Psychology, Political Behavior* and *Political Research Quarterly.* Her current projects include an evaluation of appointed boards and commissions in US cities, and a collaborative examination of gender and political socialization.

Roselyn Hsueh is Associate Professor of Political Science and co-directs the Certificate in Political Economy at Temple University. Dr Hsueh is the author of *China's Regulatory State: A New Strategy for Globalization* (2011) and scholarly articles and book chapters. She is completing a second book, *Micro-institutional Foundations of Capitalism: National Sectoral Pathways to Development,* under contract with Cambridge University Press. The *Economist, Foreign Affairs,* National Public Radio (NPR), *The Washington Post* and other media outlets have featured her research. She has testified in front of Congress and consulted for the Center for Strategic and International Studies. Dr Hsueh is on the Fulbright National Screening Committee. She has served as Global Order Visiting Scholar at the Perry World House, University of Pennsylvania, and is a member of Georgetown University's Initiative for U.S.-China Dialogue on Global Issues. Dr. Hsueh also previously served as Residential Research Faculty Fellow at the Institute of East Asian Studies and is Visiting Scholar at the Center for the Study of Law and Society, UC Berkeley and has lectured as Visiting Professor at Tecnológico de Monterrey in Mexico. Prior to arriving at Temple, she held the Hayward R. Alker Postdoctoral Fellowship at the Center for International Studies, University of Southern California, and conducted international fieldwork as a Fulbright Scholar and a David L. Boren Fellow of the National Security Education Program. She earned her bachelor's, master's and PhD from the University of California, Berkeley.

Dolores Huerta is an activist and feminist who worked alongside Cesar Chavez to help found the United Farmworkers (UFW) Union. Throughout the decades Huerta, with the UFW, has worked tirelessly to ensure that farmworkers are protected, and their rights are respected. As a testament to her organizing and lobbying talents Huerta is responsible for securing Aid for Dependent Families and disability insurance for farm workers in California. Prior to founding the UFW, she started as an organizer for the Stockton Community Service Organization (CSO) located in Northern California. During her time at CSO she founded the Agricultural Workers Association, which set up voter registration drives and mobilized local residents to lobby their local government for community improvements. These efforts took Huerta all over the country where she met many important figures who continue to influence her today. One such person is Gloria Steinem, who in part is responsible for putting Huerta on to her feminist path. As a result of her dedication to humanitarian efforts, Huerta has been awarded various honorary doctorates, and more importantly, the Presidential Medal of Freedom, which President Barack Obama conferred upon her in 2012.

Kristin Kanthak is Associate Professor of Political Science at the University of Pittsburgh. Her work centers on questions of diversity and representation in politics. Her more recent works has focused especially on women and politics, particularly on how and why women engage in representation. Her research has appeared in the *American Political Science Review*, the *American Journal of Political Science*, as well as in other outlets. She is co-editor of *State Politics and Policy Quarterly*. She is currently working on a book on research design from a research transparency perspective.

J. Celeste Lay is an associate professor of Political Science at Tulane University. She earned her Bachelor's in Political Science at the College of Charleston (1998) and her PhD in Government & Politics at the University of Maryland, College Park (2004). She is the author of *A Midwestern Mosaic: Immigration and Political Socialization in Rural America* (2012), a book about the response to immigration in small Iowa towns. Her research focuses on political socialization, voting behavior, women and politics, and attitudes about and the politics surrounding education policy. She is particularly interested in local government and how places shape attitudes and behavior. She has published in several peer-reviewed journals and serves on the board of *Urban Affairs Review*. She is also the co-director of the New Orleans chapter of the Scholars Strategy Network and works to help scholars connect their work with the media and policymakers.

Dc Lozano is a writer, community organizer and life-long hammer-wielder, swinging day and night at the patriarchy. She lives in Redlands, California, with her dogs Bula and Rodham, and her wife, Jenny. As the most qualified, Rodham is obviously the top dog in the house.

Jennifer L. Merolla is Professor of Political Science at the University of California, Riverside. She received her Bachelor's from Boston College and her Master's and PhD from Duke University. Her research focuses on how the political environment shapes individual attitudes and behavior across many domains, such as candidate evaluations during elections, immigration policy attitudes, foreign policy attitudes and support for democratic values and institutions. She is co-author of *Democracy at Risk: How Terrorist Threats Affect the Public*, published with the University of Chicago Press (2009), and *Framing Immigrants: News Coverage, Public Opinion and Policy*, published with the Russell Sage Foundation (2016). Her work has also appeared in journals such as *Comparative Political Studies, Electoral Studies*, the *Journal of Politics, Perspectives on Politics, Political Behavior, Political Research Quarterly, Political Psychology* and *Women, Politics, and Policy*. Merolla was field editor of American Political Behavior for the *Journal of Politics* from January of 2015–19. She engages the broader public through media, including writing in outlets such as CNBC, *The Hill* (Congress Blog), *The Washington Post* (Monkey Cage) and *U.S. News and World Report*.

Melissa R. Michelson is Professor of Political Science at Menlo College. Her research interests include Latinx politics, voter mobilization experiments and LGBTQ rights. Her six co-authored books include *Mobilizing Inclusion: Transforming the Electorate through Get-Out-the-Vote Campaigns* (2012) and *Listen, We Need to Talk: How to Change Attitudes about LGBT Rights* (2017). Her most recent book is *Transforming Prejudice: Fear, Identity, and Transgender Rights* (2020). She is a founding board member of Women Also Know Stuff. In her spare time, she knits and runs marathons.

Celeste Montoya is an associate professor of Women and Gender Studies at the University of Colorado Boulder. Her research focuses on the politics of gender and race in the United States, Europe and the global context. She is author of *From Global to Grassroots: The European Union, Transnational Activism, and Combating Violence against Women* (2013, 2014) and co-editor of *Gendered Mobilization and Intersectional Challenges: Contemporary Social Movements in Europe and the United States* (2019).

Tatishe M. Nteta is Associate Professor in the Department of Political Science at the University of Massachusetts, Amherst. His research is situated within the subfield of American politics and examines the impact that the sociopolitical incorporation of the nation's minority population has on public opinion, political behavior and political campaigns. His work has appeared in *Political Research Quarterly, Political Psychology, Political Communication, American Politics Research, Public Opinion Quarterly* and *Social Science Quarterly*.

Shayla C. Nunnally is an associate professor with a joint appointment in Political Science and Africana Studies Institute. She received her Master's and PhD in Political Science at Duke University. She specializes in public opinion and political behavior, race and politics, African American public opinion and political behavior and black political development. Her research interests include political socialization, racial socialization, trust, intergroup relations and attitudes, social capital and collective memory. Her research has appeared in the *Journal of Politics*, the *Journal of Black Studies*, the *Du Bois Review*, the *Journal of African American Studies*, and several encyclopedias and edited volumes. She also has a book with New York University Press, *Trust in Black America: Race, Discrimination, and Politics (2012)*, wherein she analyses black Americans' public opinion about race, political trust, social trust and racial trust. Her current research focuses on the transmission of memory across generations and communities of black Americans and what this transmission means for cultural trauma, group remembrance, group politics and institution building. She was awarded the 2009 Fannie Lou Hamer Award for Outstanding Community Service by the National Conference of Black Political Scientists. Additionally, in 2009, she was awarded the Outstanding Young Professionals Member for the Eastern Region of the National Urban League.

Torie Osborn Torie is known nationally for helping lead major fights for social justice for four decades, including the AIDS crisis, LGBTQ rights, and economic justice. Torie served as executive director of the social-justice foundation, Liberty Hill, and of Los Angeles's LGBT Center and the National Gay and Lesbian Task Force at the height of the AIDS epidemic. She has worked on progressive tax reform with California Calls, a state-wide community-organizing network increasing voter participation by young people, people of color and immigrants. She is currently top policy adviser to LA County Supervisor Sheila Kuehl, working on labor and immigrants' rights, a new Women and Girls Initiative and expanding affordable housing. She served as Deputy Mayor for LA Mayor Antonio R. Villaraigosa, overseeing the Mayor's field and civic engagement programs. In 2016, she ran a Hillary for America phone bank out of her house for six weeks and has led a group of 165 (mostly) women to Las Vegas to door-knock during get-out-the-vote week. After the election, that group, Team T.O., morphed into the ongoing *Team TO Resist and Rise!*, a
"Resistance" group with 150 active members that worked for eighteen months to register, educate and mobilize voters and helped flip two southern California Congressional Districts in 2018, CA-25 (Katie Hill) and CA-48 (Harley Rouda). Torie's roots are in 1960s activism on racism, anti-war, and women's liberation.

She is a published author and former columnist with a Bachelor's in English from Middlebury College and an MBA from UCLA's Anderson School.

Zoe M. Oxley is Professor of Political Science at Union College. She earned her A.B. in Government and Legal Studies from Bowdoin College and her Master's and PhD in Political Science from Ohio State University. She is a teacher and scholar of political behavior in the United States, with specific interests in public opinion, gender politics, political communication, and political psychology. Her research has explored the effects of the news media on the formation and content of political opinions, the role of gender stereotyping in elections for state executive offices and the transmission of partisanship from parents to their children. She is the co-author of *Public Opinion: Democratic Ideals, Democratic Practice* and *Conducting Empirical Analysis: Public Opinion in Action*. Her research has been published in *American Political Science Review, Journal of Politics, Political Research Quarterly, Politics & Gender, Political Behavior* and *PS: Political Science and Politics*.

Adrian D. Pantoja is a professor in Political Studies and Chicano Studies at Pitzer College. Prior to his appointment at Pitzer College, Pantoja was a professor at Arizona State University and the University of Connecticut. He received his PhD in Political Science from the Claremont Graduate University in 2001. His research has appeared in numerous books and academic journals including *Political Research Quarterly, Political Behavior, Social Science Quarterly, American Behavioral Scientist, Ethnic and Racial Studies, Journal of Religion and Society, Journal of Ethnic and Migration Studies* and *Journal of International Migration*. Professor Pantoja also worked as a researcher for the Tomas Rivera Policy Institute and as a consultant to the National Association of Latino Elected Officials; the California League of Conservation Voters; the legal firm Garcia, Calderon, Ruiz; and the Universidad de San Carlos in Guatemala. He is currently a senior analyst with Latino Decisions, a political polling firm surveying and analyzing the Latino electorate. He has offered expert commentary on Latino politics to *The New York Times, The Washington Times, The Christian Science Monitor, The Arizona Republic, La Opinion*, and other newspapers.

Jennifer M. Piscopo is an associate professor of Politics at Occidental College. Her research on women's political representation has appeared in twelve peer-reviewed journals, including *Social Politics, Comparative Political Studies, The Latin American Research Review* and *The Journal of Women, Politics, and Policy*. With Susan Franceschet and Mona Lena Krook, she is editor of *The Impact of Gender*

Quotas (2012). She has consulted for international organizations (including UN Women) as well as for national governments. Her op-eds have appeared in *The New York Times*, *The Washington Post*, *The Los Angeles Times* and *Ms. Magazine*, among other outlets. Prior to joining the Politics Faculty at Occidental College, she was Assistant Professor of Public Policy at Salem College from 2011 to 2013. Recently, she was the 2016–2017 Peggy Rockefeller Visiting Scholar at the David Rockefeller Center of Latin American Studies at Harvard University.

Jesse H. Rhodes is Professor of Political Science at the University of Massachusetts, Amherst. His major areas of scholarly interest are social policy, voting rights policy, economic inequality, and political behavior. His first book, on the development of federal education policy, *An Education in Politics: The Origin and Development of No Child Left Behind*, was published with Cornell University Press in 2012. His second book *Ballot Blocked: The Political Erosion of the Voting Rights Act* was published by Stanford University Press in 2017. Rhodes has also published research in *Political Research Quarterly*, the *Quarterly Journal of Economics*, *Perspectives on Politics*, *Political Behavior*, *Party Politics*, *Presidential Studies Quarterly*, the *Journal of Race, Ethnicity, and Politics*, *Polity*, and other journals.

Brinda Sarathy is Director of the Robert Redford Conservancy for Southern California Sustainability and Professor of Environmental Analysis at Pitzer College. Sarathy's scholarly and teaching interests focus on issues of environmental justice, natural resource management, and environmental policy. She has authored or edited several books including *Inevitably Toxic: Historic Perspectives on Contamination, Exposure, and Expertise* (2018), *Pineros: Latino Labour and the Changing Face of Foresty in the Pacific Northwest* (2012) and *Partnerships for Empowerment: Participatory Research for Community-Based Natural Resource Management* (2008). Her articles have appeared in the *Journal of Forestry*, *Society and Natural Resources*, *Policy Sciences*, *Race Gender & Class* and *Local Environment*. She received her PhD in Environmental Science, Policy and Management from the University of California, Berkeley.

Elizabeth (Libby) A. Sharrow is Assistant Professor in the Department of Political Science and the Department of History at the University of Massachusetts, Amherst. Her research focuses on the ways that public policy has shaped understandings of gender, race, sexuality, and class in US politics over the past fifty years, particularly through debates over Title IX of the Education

Amendments of 1972. She is currently working to complete a book manuscript on the political history of Title IX. Her work has been published in *Political Research Quarterly*, *Public Opinion Quarterly*, *Politics, Groups, and Identities*, the *Journal of Women, Policy & Politics* and *Social Science Quarterly*.

Carrie Skulley is an assistant professor of Politics at Sewanee: The University of the South. Her work focuses on representation and how historically marginalized groups gain access to government. Specifically, she seeks to understand the ways in which gender, race, ethnicity, and the intersections of these identities affect candidate emergence and subsequent electoral experiences. Her work has appeared in *Unconventional, Partisan, and Polarizing Rhetoric: How the 2016 Election Changed the Way Candidates Strategize, Engage, and Communicate, Politics Groups and Identities* and *Political Research Quarterly*.

Gloria Steinem is a writer, lecturer, political activist, and feminist organizer. She travels in the United States and other countries as an organizer and lecturer and is a frequent media spokeswoman on issues of equality. She is particularly interested in the shared origins of sex and race caste systems, gender roles, and child abuse as roots of violence, non-violent conflict resolution, the cultures of indigenous peoples and organizing across boundaries for peace and justice. She lives in New York City, and just published her first book in over twenty years.

Emma Stephens is a professor in the Economics Field Group and has been with Pitzer College since 2007 after completing her PhD in Development and Agricultural Economics at Cornell University. Her research and teaching focus on the intersections between economic development and agriculture, primarily in Sub-Saharan Africa. She has published several peer-reviewed articles examining the commodity market participation decisions of subsistence farmers, the spatial market integration patterns for commodity markets and bio-economic modeling of subsistence farming systems.

She is currently working with an interdisciplinary research team of systems modelers, crop and livestock scientists and a nutritionist on examining ways to integrate food security metrics into agricultural systems models in low- and middle-income countries, with a particular focus on the overarching themes of the role of identity and inequality on both agricultural and food security system outcomes.

In addition to teaching and conducting research, she has also recently become one of the editors-in-chief at the journal *Agricultural Systems*.

Debra Van Sickle is a recently retired a professor of mathematics at Sacramento City College, Sacramento, California. She received her Bachelor's and M.A.T from the University of California, Davis. She was past-president of the California Mathematics Council Community Colleges Foundation and co-coordinator for Sacramento City College Mathematics for the California Basic Skills Initiative. She has been an occasional on-air contributor for CBS News in Sacramento. Starting in 1974 she began volunteering in national, state, and local elections, especially in registration and get-out-the-vote efforts. She is most proud of the fact that for many years of her teaching career she taught her classes on Halloween in costume as a suffragist. She gave each class a brief history lesson on suffrage in America—including the fact that her own grandmother was born at a time when American women were not allowed to vote. She then encouraged her students to register and vote in the next election.

Rachel VanSickle-Ward is a professor of Political Studies at Pitzer College in Claremont, California. She received her Bachelor's from Pitzer College and her Master's and PhD from the University of California, Berkeley. Her research interests include public policy, public law, state politics and gender and politics. She has published work on the politics of statutory language, gender and political ambition and administrative law. Her first book, *The Devil Is in the Details: Understanding the Causes of Policy Specificity and Ambiguity* (2014; winner, Herbert A. Simon Book Award), explores the impact of political and institutional fragmentation on policy wording, focusing on the dynamics of social policy construction in the states. She is a frequent commentator on KPCC's Take Two (Southern California Public Radio). Her writing and commentary has appeared in *Talking Points Memo, The Washington Post (The Monkey Cage), U.S. News and World Report* and *TIME* magazine. She was named the 2012 Pitzer College Scholar in Residence for her research on contraception politics and policy, and she has co-authored a book on the subject, *The Politics of the Pill: Gender, Framing, and Policymaking in the Battle over Birth Control*, with Kevin Wallsten (2019).

Christina Wolbrecht is a professor of Political Science, director of the Rooney Center for the Study of American Democracy, and C. Robert and Margaret Hanley Family Director of the Notre Dame Washington Program. She is the co-author, with J. Kevin Corder, of *Counting Women's Ballots: Female Voters from Suffrage through the New Deal* (2016), which received the 2017 Victoria Schuck

Award for the Best Book on Women and Politics from the APSA. She also is the author of *The Politics of Women's Rights: Parties, Positions, and Change* (2000), which received the 2001 Leon D. Epstein Outstanding Book Award from the Political Organizations and Parties Section of the APSA. Wolbrecht has authored or co-authored articles on such topics as women as political role models, the representation of women and the partisan position-taking on education policy, and co-edited books on the American political parties, women as political actors and democratic inclusion. Her forthcoming book, with J. Kevin Corder, is *A Century of Votes for Women: American Elections Since Suffrage.*

Abby K. Wood is an associate professor of Law, Political Science and Public Policy at the Gould School of Law at University of Southern California. Her research is at the intersection of law and politics, with a particular focus on campaign finance, transparency and bureaucracy. Her work has appeared in *Journal of Empirical Legal Studies, Journal of Public Administration, Research and Theory, Election Law Journal, Political Research Quarterly,* among other journals and law reviews. From 2015 to 2017, Wood served on the Federal Bipartisan Campaign Finance Task Force. Before joining USC Gould, Wood clerked for the Honorable John T. Noonan, judge of the Court of Appeals for the Ninth Circuit. She also has consulted on good governance projects in association with USAID, World Bank, National Democratic Institute for International Affairs and UNDP.

Elizabeth (Liz) J. Zechmeister is Cornelius Vanderbilt Professor of Political Science and director of the LAPOP survey research institute at Vanderbilt University. She is a scholar of comparative political behavior and public opinion. Her research includes studies of voting, ideology, political parties, representation, charisma, and crisis. Zechmeister has received support from the *National Science Foundation* for investigations into the public opinion consequences of terrorist threat and natural disaster. She has published articles in the *American Journal of Political Science,* the *Journal of Politics, Comparative Political Studies* and *Political Behavior,* among other outlets. She is co-author of *Democracy at Risk: How Terrorist Threats Affect the Public* (2009) and *Latin American Party Systems* (2010). She is co-editor of *The Latin American Voter: Pursuing Representation and Accountability in Challenging Contexts* (2015). In 2012, she was the recipient of the Vanderbilt A&S Jeffrey Nordhaus Award for Excellence in Undergraduate Teaching and in 2015, she received the Vanderbilt Award for Excellence in Graduate Teaching.

Prologue: The Path up Is Always a Jagged Line

Gloria Steinem*

I first became aware of Hillary when she was a young attorney working with the congressional committee investigating President Richard Nixon. There were virtually no women doing what she was doing, so I remembered her name—Hillary Rodham. To this day, we've never sat down and had lunch together, but we have passed messages and shared hopes, and I suspect we feel we can depend on each other long-distance.

Hillary doesn't play the game, but the irrationality of the current political game plays her. Whenever she's been in a role for a while—for instance, in the White House or as a senator or as secretary of state—her approval ratings soar. Yet the minute she aspires to something higher, those ratings drop. The bias against women who don't play a "feminine" role could not be more obvious: Who does she think she is? How dare she aspire to something more?

Supporting Hillary in the election was an easy decision: she may have been the most experienced presidential candidate in the history of the nation, but I did recognize that if I had supported Bernie Sanders, I would have been praised by the same people who condemned me for supporting Hillary. She and Bernie shared many of the same ideas, so it wasn't as if there were a huge difference on issues. It's the fact that women who deny themselves by supporting a man are always praised more by some people than those who affirm and support a woman.

On Election Night of 2016, I was sitting with a group of female ambassadors to the UN, women from different continents, who were watching the results in New York. I could see from the faces around me that her defeat was devastating—not just in this country but worldwide. Yet I know that in the future, Hillary's defeat will be part of our victories because the path up is always a jagged line, not a straight one. Our victory is not a one-person marathon

* An earlier version of this essay first appeared in Teen Vogue in November of 2018. https://www.tee nvogue.com/story/what-gloria-steinem-learned-from-hillary-clinton-about-progress.

but a relay race. When the first of many diverse women wins this highest of all democratic offices, she will be climbing steps that were carved out by Hillary. And everyone who has been inspired by her will activate talents that might have stayed dormant without her.

From Hillary, I learned courage, calm and kindness—even when her own character was being attacked with fantastic lies. All you have to do is list the accusations against her and they fall from their own unspeakably ridiculous weight. I also learned the depth of hatred that comes when you break with centuries of hierarchy that starts with sex and race.

And above all, I learned to keep going and to stay true to oneself.

Introduction

Jennifer L. Merolla and Rachel VanSickle-Ward

Even more important than the history we make tonight, is the history we will write together in the years ahead.

Hillary Clinton, DNC victory speech[1]

There are a lot of ways to try to silence women. You can shout them down, or talk over them. You can criticize the tone of their voice; tell them to stop shouting. You can claim they are too young, or too old. You can forbid them from entering the place where the conversations happen. You can claim they don't have the credentials, or the expertise; argue that they are too emotional, question their intellect. Claim they are lying. You can threaten them with violence. Threaten their livelihood, their families. Chant "Lock her up." Call them unqualified. Call them nasty.

Or you can ignore them when they speak. Pretend it never happened. Pretend the words were said by a man. Erase the contributions. Erase the effort. And then claim, over and over again that actually, they never said anything of worth, or anything at all.

Hillary Clinton has far more privilege and power and access than the vast majority of women in the world. Yet all of these things have happened to her, in one way or another, during her career, and in some cases during her 2016 presidential campaign. All of them happen to women, in one way or another, throughout our daily lives, connected to our jobs in politics, academia, or elsewhere. Born of seeking power or change or simply our desire to speak. Sometimes the slights may seem less dramatic than the ones directed at Clinton—someone takes credit for our idea at a meeting, shouts something vulgar on the street. Sometimes the consequences are far, far more dire.[2]

Of all the attempts to silence Clinton, perhaps the most surprising is the attempted erasure. Of course, one of the most famous political figures in the world is going to be called horrible names. Of course, she will be vilified and mocked and maligned and threatened for the audacity to speak. But how do you pretend one of the most famous and outspoken political figures in the world never said much of anything? Perhaps more to the point, how do you pretend that a demonstrably inspiring icon never inspired anyone?

It turns out it's alarming easy. Say it often enough. Repeat it over and over. No message (never mind the policy-rich speeches and phrases she made famous), no enthusiasm (never mind the adoring supporters), unlikable (never mind being ranked the most admired woman a record-breaking twenty-two times), unpopular (never mind winning the popular vote). Say it often enough and people start to believe it, to repeat it is obvious, a given. *Nobody likes her.*

But of course, millions of people like her—love her even. They see themselves in her, feel inspired by her, strive to do better and make things better, because of the model that she set and the path that she forged. Some maybe even have complicated or conflicted feelings about her, as informed folks often do about elected leaders, but recognize and value the influence that she has had.

And so the attempts to erase her, her message and accomplishments, have collateral damage—if nobody likes her, then the people who keep saying they like her must not really exist. If she had no message, then the people for whom her message resonated must have imagined it. Indeed, one of the most profound ways you can try to silence a woman is by silencing those who came before her, to try to put a fence up where the path was forged.

The purpose of this volume, then, is to illuminate the path she forged. We tell the story of Clinton's enduring legacy through the voices of those who study it and those who feel it directly. In the pages that follow, contributors articulate the many dimensions of the "Hillary effect" with passion, enthusiasm, and careful analysis. While the stories told here represent a range of experiences and use a variety of methodological approaches, the collective message is that Clinton's long career in public service changed politics and policy for the better.

The chapters included in this volume highlight, unpack, and contextualize the positive impact of Hillary Clinton's career, campaigns, and continued presence in political life. In some cases, they are very personal reflections; in others, they are summations of scholarly work. We solicited contributions from a diverse group of scholars, activists, political leaders, and teachers. The focus is forthrightly positive and optimistic. Public discourse has focused extensively on her failures—real and imagined. Negative commentary specifically about her, as a candidate, a wife, a mother, a woman, has been ubiquitous both during the 2016 election and throughout her time on the public stage. Calls for her silence have been nearly constant, including in the lead up to the 2018 midterm elections and the 2020 presidential elections. This is not surprising for a number of reasons, some of which we delve into in this volume, but such discourse devalues the historic nature of her campaign and career and reinforces pernicious expectations of perfection that are harmful not just to Hillary, or women in politics, but also to women more generally. Additionally, both during and after her campaign, there has been a paucity of attention to the passion and enthusiasm of her supporters, despite the fact that she won the popular vote. We seek to remedy that gap, to amplify and better understand the perspectives of those who support and admire her.

There is critique of Clinton's campaign and career that is valid, thoughtful, and necessary; some of these chapters touch on that critique and provide meaningful context. Other criticisms are steeped in misogynistic tropes; chapters included here address those head on as well. But by in large this book is intended to shine a light on how Clinton, despite incredible obstacles, has succeeded. These are stories of accomplishments, gratitude, resilience, inspiration, and hope.

One tangible impact is the extent to which Clinton has inspired women to run for political office. As contributor ("A Year After") A'shanti F. Gholar, political director of Emerge America, states, in describing a surge of female candidates after the 2016 election, "A lot of people are calling all these women running for office the 'Trump Effect.' I disagree with that. I call it the 'Hillary effect.'"[3] Professor Kanthak's chapter in this volume further reinforces this point; she discusses recent research in which she was able to isolate a Hillary effect in increasing political ambition among women positively disposed toward her.

As the contributions of this volume will show, the "Hillary effect" extends well beyond women throwing their hats into the ring to run for political office. In Part 1, we focus on what Clinton has meant to women in their daily lives, an area greatly under-explored in both public and academic spaces. How did observing such a highly qualified woman run for the highest office in the United States, with all of the trials and tribulations along the way, shape women's own sense of self, priorities, and personal ambitions? There are several compelling takeaways from these pieces; the authors explain how Clinton's example helped them overcome imposter syndrome, recognize the power of their own voice, look past media caricatures and look carefully to see others because they had been seen. Overall, the Hillary effect gleaned from these accounts is one of resilience, recognition, and resistance against the voices that tell women not to strive.

In Part 2 of the volume, we explore Clinton's role in shaping activism. Her groundbreaking campaign in 2008 set the stage for igniting a sense of hope and possibility in the 2016 race, from young girls looking for role models to mothers of those girls looking for a leader to emulate, to senior women hoping to see the first woman president. Women across the generational divide, from different walks of life, became more active in politics as a result of Clinton's historic run, as well as her loss to Donald Trump. The contributions put women's activism into historical perspective. This section includes words of wisdom from civil rights icon Dolores Huerta and Jenn Carson, an organizer for Pantsuit Nation. There is also discussion in other contributions on how Clinton's candidacy and unexpected loss led in part to the inaugural Women's March in 2017, the single largest protest demonstration in US history. Additional contributors reflect on how the personal and emotional grip of the 2016 election has helped women find their voices for the first time, or as a life-long activist notes, helped them rediscover their power. A final contribution in this section also reflects on how Clinton's campaign was shaped by activists in the Black Lives Matter movement.

Part 3 of the volume examines Clinton's impact on campaigns and elections. The section unpacks how the evolution of Clinton's campaigns over the years helps us to understand some of the challenges and opportunities that women candidates face in running for the highest office of the land, and how her successes and failures in the campaign arena have had important downstream consequences. Some contributors speak to how Clinton motivated them to seek electoral office, and how Clinton helped them see that being a woman is not a liability but is rather an asset. Other contributors reflect on Clinton as a candidate: how Clinton was mindful of the importance of the inclusivity of traditionally underrepresented communities in her campaigns, such as the Latina/o community in American politics. Another set of contributors highlight her approach of being unapologetically female as a presidential candidate. Unlike her first run in 2008, in 2016 she embraced her womanhood resulting in the enhancement of an influential legacy. A final group of contributors discuss how Clinton was able to combat some of the more negative stereotypes that she faced on the campaign trail.

The significance of role models like Hillary Clinton is less well documented in scholarship when it comes to children, so Part 4 examines the effect Clinton has had on children and families. In a piece in the Monkey Cage during the election (and adapted in this volume), Wolbrecht and Campbell reflect on how Clinton's run will likely increase political engagement among young women.[4] The other contributions in this part pick up on that idea and speak to the influence Clinton has had on young children, older children and the parents of those children. The contributions include ambitious research programs that surveyed and interviewed over 1500 elementary school kids after the 2016 election, as well as personal reflections on how the presence of Clinton and her campaign influenced young girls, older girls, and their mothers. The contributions also look at the impact of the election on fathers of first daughters, drawing from survey research during the election.

As someone who has been a public servant for decades in multiple roles, and as someone with a reputation for being a policy wonk, we would be remiss not to consider the myriad ways that Clinton has influenced policy. Part 5 therefore speaks to Clinton's policymaking influence, both from a domestic and from an international perspective. The contributors consider her multilateral approach to foreign policy, as well as her championing the interests of women and girls in the international arena, long before it was politically popular to do so. Other contributors look at the important work Clinton has done in the domestic arena on voting rights for marginalized communities. They also counter claims that Clinton lacked an economic message in the 2016 election, and instead showcase her message, which not only spoke about the economy generally but also highlighted economic challenges faced by women. The final contribution in the policy section speaks to the value of Clinton's approach to policymaking, which marries expertise with the lived experiences of individuals, in particular among women.

While there is much to say about Clinton's impact across the dimensions we cover in this volume—policy, activism, ambition, campaigns and elections, parents and kids—the true effect of Clinton's influence is yet unfolding, because it exists in the countless stories of those whose lives she touched. This volume gives voice to some of those stories and provides research to back them up. In short, we explain how the "Hillary Effect" reverberates beyond one campaign or election and provides a window into abiding lessons in American politics.

Part One

"I'm With Her": Clinton's Impact on Women's Lives and Ambitions

Preface

Jennifer L. Merolla

We are the ones we have been waiting for.

—June Jordan

From defying traditional roles of a First Lady, to declaring women's rights are human rights, to being the first woman to win a major party nomination for president, Hillary Clinton has broken down barriers to gender equality both at home and abroad. Through her service and example, she has recognized the importance of putting oneself forward and taking risks. She has done this not because it was easy, far from it. Rather, she has done this because of her desire, passion, and determination to give women a voice and more equal footing in society. As she argued at the Vital Voices conference in Vienna in 1997:

> There cannot be true democracy unless women's voices are heard. There cannot be true democracy unless women are given the opportunity to take responsibility for their own lives. There cannot be true democracy unless all citizens are able to participate fully in the lives of their country.[1]

How did watching a high profile (arguably the highest profile woman political figure in the world), hyper qualified candidate, over the course of her career and campaign, shape women's own ambition, priorities, and sense of self? The significance of role models is well documented in political science.[2] According to theories of descriptive representation, seeing members of one's group represented in political office can lead to a sense of political empowerment, and spur political engagement (Bobo and Gilliam 1990). A number of scholars have explored how the presence of women in elected office affects the political engagement of women. Some scholars have found that women come to have greater interest in politics, feel that leaders are more responsive to them and are more likely to participate when they are represented by a woman in office (Hansen 1997; High-Pippert and Comer 1998; Reingold and Harrell 2010). These effects even occur when women are present on the ballot (Hansen 1997;

Wolbrecht and Campbell 2007).[3] Most of these effects have only been explored at the congressional level, given the dearth of female candidates at the presidential level (prior to the 2020 presidential election). Furthermore, for all of this rich scholarship, existing research has not considered what the presence of women candidates, and reaction to that presence, has meant to women in their daily lives. The chapters in this section tackle these questions.

We argue that an important, and overlooked, effect of Hillary Clinton is how she has served as a role model to other women, even outside of the domain of politics. Her presence in politics, and reactions to that presence, even in the face of a devastating loss in the 2016 election, has led women to reflect on their own roles as they go about their daily lives and engage in the political world. The contributors in this section speak to the many ways in which Clinton and her experiences have transformed understandings of women's presence across different institutional settings, and have helped inspire them to take action to bring about change. According to the contributors in this section, her journey, her spirit and resilience, her fights, including successes and failures, have opened eyes, ignited hope, provided strength, caused us to dig deeper, to want more, to fight for more, even after being knocked down.

Jennifer Piscopo, an associate professor of political science, speaks of her journey to study women's representation in Latin America, which began at Clinton's alma mater, Wellesley. Drawing from her expertise on representation, she discusses how two narratives in 2016—that women only supported Clinton because she is a woman, and that she is widely disliked—deny women their rights to representation. With respect to the first narrative, Piscopo argues that it neglects that these women see in Clinton their own "struggles, stories and ambitions." The second narrative ignores the enthusiasm held among many of her supporters.

Contrary to the problematic narratives in media coverage, Piscopo notes that Clinton inspired women to want more, to demand more, to effect the change they believe is needed. So, they did not just turn out in 2016, but donated to the Clinton campaign, and after her defeat, they did not stay home, but harnessed their anger into action by marching, engaging and running for office in record numbers. And, as the other contributions in this section show, Clinton's example also inspired them to want more and to demand more in their own lives.

Debra Van Sickle, a retired math teacher, takes us further back in time, and speaks of growing up in the "same America" as Clinton and becoming inspired during the presidential election of 1992, of the promise of getting "two for the price of one." She was inspired by seeing a First Lady buck traditional gender roles, and angered by the backlash in the press. She speaks of her admiration for Clinton being linked to her complicated and nuanced life, relationships and accomplishments. The disjuncture between Clinton's words and actions and how they are covered in the press has inspired her to "dig deeper to find the truth about events and people."

Kathleen Feeley, a professor of History at the University of Redlands, brings us to Clinton's next major milestone, running for a US Senate seat in New York, and how her run inspired women. Feeley recounts how Clinton was criticized for being a carpetbagger, since she was not from New York, but turned that "disadvantage" into an advantage, by going on a listening tour of the state: "The listening tour embodied the doggedness, earnestness, intellectual engagement, and feminist values—so often used to demean and dismiss Clinton—that have long inspired supporters." She discusses the enthusiasm of women for Clinton during this election, even in parts of the state that were traditionally less Democratic. She also reflects on how Clinton's resilience and example during that election inspired her to "stay the course and do the hard work" of finishing her dissertation, even in the presence of obstacles.

Jennifer Chudy, now an assistant professor of Political Science at Wellesley College, remembers her interactions with Hillary Clinton when she was an intern in her New York Senate office. She recounts how those interactions inspired her to be an attentive mentor. In a domain in which interns are often invisible, Chudy reflects on how being "seen" by Clinton was transformative, making her feel valued and heard. That experience was important in her own trajectory and in how she engages with her students. As a professor at Clinton's alma mater, an all-women's college, she also reflects on how Clinton has inspired her students, not only through her example as a public servant but also in her "strength and resilience." She encourages their desire for more by seeing and supporting their potential, the way that Clinton did for her.

The last two contributions take us more deeply into the 2016 election and how women see in Clinton their own stories, struggles, and resilience. Rabbi Jaclyn Cohen reveals how Clinton's "path-blazing presidential campaign and stunning defeat," coupled with Cohen's own entry into motherhood and all that goes with it, opened her eyes to how most of her life was spent "accommodating men." While Clinton's defeat was devastating to herself and her congregation, she notes that it may also serve as an important wake-up call for more of us to stand up in our personal and professional lives.

Brinda Sarathy, professor of Environmental Studies, poignantly reflects on her days in graduate school, of feeling like an imposter, feeling invisible, being mansplained to by "Theory Bros," but surviving by being resilient and building supportive networks, and of going on to do the gendered service labor that is often performed by women faculty. These experiences are familiar to many women in male-dominated fields. Like many other contributors in this section, Clinton's loss was painful, was personal and yet, motivating. Sarathy is now louder, more engaged, both in her career and in political life. She has embraced June Jordan's empowering words "we are the ones we have been waiting for."

References

Bobo, L. and F. D. Gilliam (1990), "Race, Sociopolitical Participation, and Black Empowerment," *American Political Science Review*, 84 (2): 377–93.

Dolan, K. (2006), "Symbolic Mobilization? The Impact of Candidate Sex in American Elections," Working papers. Institute of Government Studies, University of California at Berkeley, http://escholarship.org/uc/item/2qp5d81k.

Hansen, S. B. (1997), "Talking About Politics: Gender and Contextual Effects in Political Proselytizing," *Journal of Politics*, 59: 73–103.

High-Pippert, A. and J. Comer (1998), "Female Empowerment: The Influence of Women Representing Women," *Women and Politics*, 19: 53–66.

Lawless, J. (2004), "Politics of Presence? Congresswomen and Symbolic Representation," *Political Research Quarterly*, 57: 81–99.

Reingold, B. and J. Harrell (2010), "The Impact of Descriptive Representation on Women's Political Engagement: Does Party Matter?," *Political Research Quarterly*, 63: 280–94.

Wolbrecht, C. and D. E. Campbell (2007), "Leading By Example: Female Members of Parliament as Political Role Models," *American Journal of Political Science*, 51: 921–39.

The Stories Not Told

Misrepresenting the Women Who Loved Clinton

Jennifer M. Piscopo

I did not attend Wellesley College because of Hillary Clinton—at least not consciously. I didn't want to go to a women's college. In retrospect, my reluctance made no sense, because my teenage self was a feminist, even if lacking the academic vocabulary of feminism. I felt both rage and grief because my grandfather prevented my mother from going to college. A voracious reader of novels, I only read books by women authors that featured women heroines.

It was 1998. Clinton's comment about staying at home and baking cookies was years past, but frequently resurrected in the media. I remember thinking, "Of course she wouldn't want to stay home, that sounds boring." Whatever the story of my life would be, like Clinton and the heroines of my novels, I wanted *more*.

In the end, I chose Wellesley. A prospective student visit showed me what happened when smart women came together without limitations. The banners said, "Women who will make a difference in the world." Wellesley groomed us for excellence. No subjects, careers, or ambitions were off limits. At some earlier point, I had received the message that math and science wasn't for girls. At Wellesley, a woman Astronomy professor said to me, "But you are really good at solving these problems." My self-understanding turned upside down. Each day was a lesson in how gender stereotypes shape the limits of the possible, and how role models undo these norms.

I minored in Astronomy, but united my interests in global affairs, political science, and women's studies by majoring in Latin American Studies. Women played significant roles in the civil wars, social movements and democratization processes that shaped Latin American politics in the 1980s and 1990s (Jaquette

1994). Since I was born after the heyday of second wave feminism in the United States—and the US women's movement remained absent from my high school history books—Latin America drew my attention for the sheer numbers of women in public roles. At the same time, I was thrilled to share a Wellesley connection with Hillary Clinton and Madeleine Albright, women who broke barriers closer to home.

My career became dedicated to understanding women's political representation: how and when women attain political power, and why it matters. When political scientists talk about *political representation*, they mean more than just choosing legislators from a certain district. Representation also means feeling seen and feeling included. People in office need to resemble the people they represent, in terms of their identity and their lived experiences (Phillips 1998). I focused on Latin America, where some countries elect legislatures comprised of over 40 percent women.[1] I obtained my PhD in political science, joined the faculty at an elite liberal arts college, published my research and began consulting for organizations like UN Women.

So by 2016, I had the feminist vocabulary to understand *exactly* what made media coverage of Clinton's campaign elicit that familiar mix of rage and grief. Two media narratives in particular left me seething: that women supported Hillary just because they wanted a woman president, and that voters did not like her.

These narratives deny women their rights to political representation. Clinton's career encapsulated the struggles, stories, and ambitions of so many women. She faced relentless sexism and countless setbacks, and still she triumphed. She dedicated herself to public service. At the 1995 World Conference on Women in Beijing, she acted against advice and declared, "Women's rights are human rights." Like many other feminists, I looked at Clinton, and I said *her*. Not some random woman to be the first president, but *her*, because her fights are also our fights. She would represent the countless American women who chose not to stay home, either.

As the media spilt endless ink asking why voters liked Trump, they ignored the women who rallied behind Clinton. The assumption that no one liked Clinton was never seriously challenged, even as her campaign upended the conventional political science wisdom about American women as voters and citizens.

Typically, women donate less money than men (Ford 2011). Women participate in electoral politics less than men (Ford 2011). Clinton changed all this: her presidential bid was bankrolled by women donors, staffed by women, and supported by women volunteers across the country.[2] Women of all ages, ethnicities, backgrounds, and religions waited in line for hours, even overnight, just to see her. I waited too, after the election: seven hours in line, eating nothing but granola bars and wearing my Wellesley sweatshirt, just to shake her hand and say "thank you." Thank you for wanting and for demanding *more*.

Women's underrepresentation in political life is not new. Yet the erasure of Clinton supporters from the national narrative, especially the erasure of her women supporters, shocked even me, a scholar who understands how systematic gender bias works. The tropes about women voters as irrational—used a century ago to deny women the vote—had appeared again. Women supporting Clinton were emotional. We were kneejerk feminists who just wanted a woman president. We could not possibly be discerning voters who saw in Clinton a pragmatic and experienced politician, one who would represent our concerns and champion equality and justice.

For these reasons, Clinton's defeat feels like a personal message to all her supporters. *Your stories do not matter. Your lived experiences do not matter. You cannot have real power.* Women could break smaller barriers—become a lawyer, a senator and a secretary of state. But the highest and most powerful political office would remain the preserve of men.

Yet true to form, Clinton does not believe in surrender. Speaking to Wellesley's Class of 2017, she said, "Well I think there's only one answer, to keep going. Don't be afraid of your ambition, of your dreams, or even your anger—those are powerful forces. But harness them to make a difference in the world."[3] Unsurprisingly, Democratic women did just that following Clinton's defeat. Record numbers of women marched, engaged in civil action and ran for and won political offices across the country.

I no longer need to look to Latin America to see women filling the public sphere. With coauthors, I now research women's political representation in the United States. We designed a series of survey experiments to show that "all male panels"—legislative committees without any women—erode citizens' perceptions of democratic legitimacy (Clayton, O'Brien, and Piscopo 2019). Inspired by 2018's wave of women candidates, we have extended this research to reveal how women's exclusion shapes their political ambition.

Clinton, me, the women politicians I study—we all want more. In 2016, our voices were erased and our stories were not told, but we are fighting back. After all, Clinton taught us that we can defy the odds, challenge the stereotypes and change the ending of the story.

References

Clayton, A., D. Z. O'Brien and J. M. Piscopo (2019), "All Male Panels? Representation and Democratic Legitimacy," *American Journal of Political Science*, 63 (1): 113–29.

Ford, L. E. (2011), *Women & Politics: The Pursuit of Equality*, Boston: Wadsworth.

Friedman, Megan (2017), "The Women of Hillary Clinton's Campaign are Not Done Fighting," *Cosmopolitan*, January 19.

Jaquette, J., ed. (1994), *The Women's Movement in Latin America: Participation and Democracy*, Boulder: Westview Press.

Phillips, A. (1998), *The Politics of Presence*, New York: Oxford University Press.

Zhou, Li (2016), "Hillary Clinton's Women Donors Could Change Politics Forever," *The Atlantic*, January 30.

2

Parallel Lives

Debra Van Sickle

After I voted that November morning in 2016, I asked someone to take a picture of me with my "I voted" sticker affixed to the pants suit I wore for the occasion. In the months before the election, a friend and I waited in line in the hot sun for hours to hear Hillary speak, I flew to the other side of the state to campaign with my daughter and drove hundreds of miles to a neighboring state to do so with my son. I began making plans to attend the inauguration. I was more passionate in my support for Hillary than I had ever been for anyone else running for office in the over four decades I have been active in politics. In California we knew fairly early in the evening on Election Day 2016 that although Hillary was going to win a few million more votes, she was going to lose in the Electoral College. I was devastated. I couldn't watch or listen to the returns; I just went to bed. This was not just about policy, or about having a Democrat in the White House. The pain was something more akin to the pain I felt when a dear friend had died about a year before. I felt that I personally had lost something, someone, really precious.

Hillary Rodham and I literally grew up in the same America. In 1957, when I was three years old, my family moved to Chicago. My dad had recently been discharged from the Navy and used his GI Bill benefits to attend the DeVry Technical Institute on Belmont Avenue. This was less than nine miles from ten-year-old Hillary's home on Wisner Street in the Chicago suburb of Park Ridge. By the early 1960s, Hillary and I were both getting our early religious education from the Methodists. Hillary attended First United in Park Ridge; my family attended Saint Steven's in Oakland, California. We both would be greatly influenced by the radical, yet biblical call being made in churches across the country for social justice. When she was fourteen, Hillary's youth pastor took her to hear Martin Luther King in Chicago. Just a few years later I was in a small group at my church in Concord, California, talking to a member of the

Black Panthers about the "Black Manifesto," a call for churches and synagogues to make 500 million dollars in reparations to African Americans in response to the devastation caused by centuries of slavery and racism.

In the fall of 1975, Hillary and I both got married and we bucked the strong tradition of taking our husband's name. Hillary chose to keep the name given to her at birth, my husband and I chose to hyphenate our last names. In the early 1980s, Hillary Rodham began to use the name Hillary Clinton (or sometimes Hillary Rodham Clinton), perhaps to help her husband win back the governorship of Arkansas. A couple of years later, after my marriage ended, I went back to using just my own last name.

I was already a single working mother of two teenagers in late 1991 and early 1992 when I actually first heard and saw Hillary. I was immediately taken with her and with the idea her husband, then running for president, put forward that if he were elected, America would get "two for the price of one." Like many others, I had spent hours during the fall of 1991 watching an all-white male senate judiciary panel grill Anita Hill when she reluctantly came forward to testify under oath that Supreme Court nominee Clarence Thomas had sexually harassed her. It became clear that the leadership of our country could not fairly represent the interests of women as long as it stayed a "boy's club." I think Hillary inspired and excited me so much because I saw her as the first woman who would have a seat at the table of power who, like me, had come of age at a time when many women were just starting to believe that with enough hard work and dedication we could "have it all": family, personal life and meaningful work that paid us well. Bill Clinton's cabinet, advisers and other staff were said to be the first that "looked like America" by including a significant number of women, people of color and people from the gay community in various rolls. Hillary was going to be the person who "looked" like me.

I remember the January 26, 1992 interview on the CBS news show "60 Minutes" in which Hillary and Bill addressed challenges in their marriage, trying to put the stories to rest before they derailed Bill's run for president. At this time I was just a few years past my own divorce. I loved Hillary's fiery response to the interviewer's suggestion that the Clintons had an "arrangement." She shot back with, "You know, I'm not sitting here, some little woman standing by my man like Tammy Wynette. . . . I'm sitting here because I love him, and I respect him, and I honor what he's been through and what we've been through together. And you know, if that's not enough for people, then heck—don't vote for him."[1] I still have some of the headbands I wore for a while after watching her in that interview. I also remember her answer to a reporter's questions about her work at an Arkansas law firm while Bill was governor: "I suppose I could have stayed home, baked cookies and had teas."[2] I was thrilled. When I would later read highly critical press accounts, including mockery of her hair, wardrobe, voice, and laugh, I was infuriated. I started to see what her extremely loyal friends and colleagues always knew: the Hillary often portrayed in all forms of public media is a caricature.

I have never really understood the disdain for a woman who, in my mind, has so often sought to use her privilege and power in the service of those with less privilege. The list of Hillary's accomplishments and initiatives is long and most often happened in collaboration with others. I have been particularly inspired by the Children's Health Insurance Program (CHIP), the Clinton foundation's work to bring lower cost HIV/AIDS treatment to nine million people worldwide and the Global Alliance for Clean Cookstoves, which has worked to replace open flame cooking that harms both the environment and the health of woman and girls. These examples are complicated and not without controversy. But real people's lives have been saved by each of these efforts. Hillary worked to get the best results possible, in messy real world situations.

My admiration of Hillary Rodham Clinton has come based on, not despite of, how complicated and imperfect her life, relationships, and accomplishments have been. I have watched her work tirelessly and speak out with passion, humor and grace, often in service of those who have little or no voice, while forces on the left and the right sought to silence her. She has taught me to dig deeper to find the truth about events and people and to use media portrayal as a starting point only, because that is what we all had to do to get to know her. I didn't get to go to her inaugural. But in the fall of 2017 my family and I went to hear her speak about the election. Reflecting on the enthusiasm of the crowd, I realized that though the pain of the loss was real, the power of her continued legacy is real too.

3

Listening Her Way to a Historic Victory

On Hillary Clinton's 1999–2000 Senate Campaign

Kathleen A. Feeley*

The media, political allies and enemies, and even long-time supporters charged Hillary Rodham Clinton (I refer to her as HRC throughout this chapter) with being "a carpetbagger, political opportunist, political novice, and political celebrity with a questionable marriage" in the months before, during and after her July 1999 announcement of a proposed Senate run (Parry-Giles 2014: 171).[1] As a native New Yorker, long-time HRC supporter and feminist scholar, my initial reaction to the possibility—and then reality—of her candidacy was excitement tempered with dread. I worried,

> We are too close to your husband's impeachment process. The Right will crucify you. The media will pillory you. You are asking too much to be the first First Lady to run for public office and the first female senator in New York State's federal delegation. You don't understand New York State politics and will focus—to your detriment—on the New York metropolitan region and won't play in upstate New York.

I, like many, wondered if she had finally gone too far. But, in this instance—as in so many others—HRC refused to be a good, quiet, unambitious girl and accept the status quo. Instead she—with great success—did what male politicians have always done: used her resources, built networks, and played to win. Her brilliant, if much-derided, campaign strategy was her listening tour of New York State, particularly in the deeply purple regions of central and western New York. Her visits—including town halls; unmediated q and a's; small group meetings— to struggling, rust-belt cities like my hometown of Utica changed hearts and minds and solidified existing support, including that of my white, working-class

* Thanks to Richard K. Feeley and Monique Peterson for their thoughtful reading of this essay.

mother who had long felt marginalized and uninspired by the overwhelmingly male politicians—Democrat and Republican alike—she'd experienced at the local, state, and national level. We found the possibility of HRC's candidacy thrilling and liberating but also dangerous. I carefully checked my enthusiasm, depending upon my audience, given the vitriol Clinton has long inspired in often otherwise reasonable people. Of course, she was a flawed candidate: who is not, particularly someone actively campaigning and/or serving in public office for as long as she did. Indeed, she could have easily failed in this endeavor. Yet she decisively won with more than 55 percent of the vote. And she did so as a woman, as a feminist and with a listening tour as a tool for progressive change.

My own state of mind in mid-1999 drove my initial, conflicted response. As a graduate student, I needed to complete my dissertation and find a full-time job. My professional prospects were tenuous, my personal life was in absolute shambles: my father fell ill and died at the same time my own long-term, live-in relationship ended. As a first-generation, working-class, female college student, my ever-present anxieties about my credibility and life plan boiled over: Had I over-reached? Was I too political, too feminist? I wanted to hide and I wanted HRC to hide. She did not and I did not. Her audacity, persistence, imperfections and intellectual and cultural ambitions helped me to stay the course and do the hard work.

Clinton's tour worked for many reasons. With it, she acknowledged a central shortcoming and set out to resolve it: she had never lived in the state (to the haters, she moved to Chappaqua, New York, in 2000 and remains there) and thus could not understand its social, political, economic, geographic, and spatial diversity nor adequately represent its citizens. She could have educated herself at a superficial remove. Instead she crisscrossed what was then the third most populous state in the nation, visiting all sixty-two counties. The tour introduced her in a new way to residents and was used to develop campaign messaging and draft policy positions that reflected New York's heterogeneous population and complex economic and political realities. As an outsider who wanted to become an insider, her campaign successfully encouraged voters—including this one—to "consider who and what they might become" (Cos and Snee 2001: 2026). This months-long project officially began with the announcement held at retiring Senator Daniel Patrick Moynihan's upstate New York farm (she did not officially declare until early February 2000). From the start, HRC and her staff demonstrated a nimble grasp of the state's abiding regional dichotomy: the real and perceived commonalities and differences as well as entrenched hostility and suspicion between downstate (New York City and its sprawling metropolitan region east to Long Island and north to Poughkeepsie) and upstate (not New York City, north and west of Poughkeepsie) New York.[2] She reached many upstate voters who felt (often justifiably) ignored by and alienated from a largely downstate-oriented modern Senate delegation. HRC also galvanized a female constituency across geographic, economic, racial, and religious lines—particularly in the conservative precincts of upstate New York—who hungered for representation. These supporters also were thrilled as she claimed her own voice and distinct role after years of diminishing herself to fit as "wife of" a governor and then a president.

The listening tour embodied the doggedness, earnestness, intellectual engagement, and feminist values—so often used to demean and dismiss Clinton—that have long inspired supporters. Doing that tour, HRC banished my early misgivings—as well those of many others; she conceded that she was a carpetbagger but turned it into a strength. She worked hard, embraced her adopted state and then used all her skills and resources to advance the interests of all New Yorkers. As someone born and raised in upstate New York who moved downstate to Brooklyn as a young adult, I lived on a regional fault line with divided loyalties. HRC was the first politician I encountered who reflected the best of that dichotomy rather than positioning herself in a particular camp. This extended listening tour and campaign showcased distinctive, gendered political skills: a willingness to listen, to adjust, to concede, and to be wary. As the tour continued into early February 2000, many grew impatient, judging her too cautious, too womanly in her reserve. But she persisted. And won. In so doing, she gave hope to voters who still want neither to be wooed nor to be shouted at, but talked to as reasonable adults who find hard work, preparation, caution, and self-reflection appealing and desirable traits for an elected official.

References

Anderson, K. V. (2002), "From Spouses to Candidates: Hillary Rodham Clinton, Elizabeth Dole, and the Gendered Office of U.S. President," *Rhetoric & Public Affairs*, 5 (1): 105–32.

Cos, G. C. and B. J. Snee (2001), "'New York, New York': Being and Creating Identity in the 2000 New York State Senate Race," *The American Behavioral Scientist*, 44 (12): 2014–29.

Parry-Giles, S. J. (2014), *Hillary Clinton in the News: Gender and Authenticity in American Politics*, Urbana: University of Illinois Press.

Scharrer, E. (2002), "'An 'Improbable Leap': A Content Analysis of Newspaper Coverage of Hillary Clinton's Transition from First Lady to Senate Candidate," *Journalism Studies*, 3 (3): 393–406.

Wolvin, A. D. (2005), "Listening Leadership: Hillary Clinton's Listening Tour," *International Journal of Listening*, 19 (1): 29–38.

Recognition

Jennifer Chudy

It is that time of the semester when students must commit to a term project. In this political science class, students will use data from the 2016 election and statistical techniques to answer a question of their choosing. I've asked students to come to class today to share their ideas. After a few announcements, we begin to go around the room. Without exception, it is clear that every student has done her homework. As each student speaks, she displays her own brand of thoughtful and earnest curiosity. There is no other word to describe it—it is inspiring, inspiring to watch their blossoming intellects on display. And as I listen to these sixteen bright students share their ideas, a clear pattern begins to emerge—the majority of them have questions about Hillary Clinton.

I can relate to their fascination with her. When I was their age, I was similarly captivated by Hillary Clinton—intelligent, resilient, ambitious! Someone who committed herself to public service, to understanding people and policies, to enduring in the face of setbacks. She inspired me from afar for years.

She became an even more inspirational figure up close. On a whim, I took all of my admiration for her and stuffed it into an internship application brimming with idealism and ambition. I was shocked to be interviewed, dumbfounded when they offered me the position and bewildered when I finally walked through the doors of her NYC District office in the summer of 2003.

Former employees often remark that, as a boss, Clinton inspires through her sincerity, humility, and thoughtfulness—I wholeheartedly concur. I can think of many episodes that illustrate these traits. For example, as part of my work for the summer, I provided background research for a report on brownfield redevelopment. After a few weeks of hard work, my supervisor Eric submitted the multi-page report to the Senator and, as is customary, had included a footnote at the bottom of the first page reading: "Intern Jennifer Chudy provided research assistance on this report."

When the report came back to us, I flipped through it, absorbing the many notes lining the margins. Notes that she had written! She read our stuff! More shocking was the lone comment on the first page. By the footnote, a circle was scrawled over my name, with a brief note scribbled next to it: "Thank you for your help, Jennifer." The rest of her comments were more substantive and technical and I am sure that I thought about them at some point, but in the moment, her small gesture, a gesture of recognition, astonished me. To be seen is a powerful experience. To be seen by someone of Clinton's stature was, for me, a transformative experience. I had a newfound confidence that my work was valued—that *I* was valued—by an intelligent and busy person. Before and since then, I have worked for public figures at all levels of government—none have taken the time to acknowledge a lowly intern in this simple but meaningful way.

I came to realize that this was a common trait of hers; she has the uncanny ability to make people feel seen and heard.[1] The most vivid and memorable incident occurred when I spent the 2003 Northeast Blackout with her. When our entire office was evacuated onto the balmy streets of midtown Manhattan one hot August day (and after being assured that there was no threat to national security), Clinton came to find us—her interns—and stuck around to answer every question, oblige in every photo request and even listen to an intern sing a song for her, until she was finally whisked away into her dowdy van.

I think about this exceptional patience and decency a lot in my current role as a professor. Once during a marathon grading session, I realized that, buried in a footnote, a student had come out to me in her assignment. She had been providing examples of variation in LGBTQ acceptance, and, to make her point, she offered the observation that she and her girlfriend faced critical stares or worse when they walked around holding hands in her home state. I paused when I read this—was this just an irrelevant aside? Or something more? Deciding it was the latter, I added a comment acknowledging this student and her experiences— I had decided to *see* her. I learned the power of recognition from Clinton.

At Wellesley, Clinton's influence is unique. Clinton inspired many of these students to study political science here and to pursue their educations driven by a real sense of purpose. Perhaps any beloved alum could impact students in these ways, but I think Hillary Clinton's influence reaches deeper. Students tell me that they see Wellesley's motto "Non Ministrari sed Ministrare" (Not to be ministered unto, but to minister) exemplified in her. One student told me: "She's *so* Wellesley. She does her homework, works really hard, and genuinely wants to help people." Perhaps that explains their preoccupation with her on this assignment; they see themselves so clearly in her example.

But to many, she is more than an exemplary public servant. Instead, it is her personal traits—strength and resilience—that students find most admirable. One student told me, "She has fought for a seat at the table for years and has withstood an unimaginable amount of hateful words and criticism. And despite all of this, she just kept forging ahead." When students tell me that they are undeterred by the current political climate and are steadfastly committed to a career in public service, I see Clinton's determination thriving among the students of her alma mater. It is my goal to encourage this drive the best way I know how: by *seeing* the students and acknowledging them as the valuable and powerful individuals that they are.

Clarity in the Chaos

A New (and Improved) Vision of Motherhood, Faith, and Feminism

Jaclyn Cohen

I spent most of my life accommodating men.

It took Hillary's path-blazing presidential campaign and its stunning conclusion for me to realize it.

As a woman rabbi, I chose to enter a field dominated by men for thousands of years. Early on I rarely, if ever, considered this. My generation of Reform Jews has only ever known a time when both women and men could be rabbis, and so I was educated within highly progressive communities—congregations that ostensibly spoke with fluency the sacred language of egalitarianism. My parents taught me from a young age I could do or be anything I set my mind to; every avenue in the world waited, wide open and eager, for *me*.

How little I knew of the battles fought long before I was even born.

How limited was my perception of my own ambition and drive.

How different it all looked through the real-time unfolding of the 2016 election.

Well, that—and my unique entry to motherhood at the very same time.

My husband and I each longed to become parents; in those early weeks of dating, articulating our shared desire for a family kicked our relationship into "serious" territory real fast. We found out I was pregnant in the spring of 2015 and, like many prospective parents, the magnitude of our combined excitement and trepidation was monumental.

Our son was born, the universe shifted—at first, in all the predictable ways. But as time wore on, it became clear to my husband that something deep and dark was plaguing me, eventually landing us in the emergency room on a bitterly cold Seattle evening. My diagnosis: severe postpartum depression. The treatment: all-encompassing.

Looking back, those early days of parenthood nearly shattered us. As overjoyed as we were to expand our family—and to hold in our arms a healthy child—we abruptly found ourselves living in a totally different reality than what we'd pictured. From a massive increase in anticipated medical expenses to an all-too-familiar stigma around mental health to the realization that we could not, in fact, do this all on our own and needed—by God, we *needed*—significant help to get through it all, so little played out like we'd planned.

And then there was this *thing*, this up-until-that-point-in-my-life totally unfamiliar reckoning around the politics of gender, human bodies, their capabilities and limitations. Pregnancy, a traumatic labor and delivery, the nightmare that was breastfeeding, the expectations and assumptions pushed upon me as "the mommy"; it felt as though each hour held a new, stunning reality around my womanhood.

In spite of all this, I was lucky. And privileged. I had twelve weeks of paid leave during which I could recover in private, away from the eyes of congregants and colleagues.

I got better. I returned to work.

But I was never the same.

As my journey through this new chapter of being a human woman unfolded, Hillary's campaign was kicking into high gear. The socialist with grand visions and limited concrete plans was growing louder. The schoolyard bully with no experience whatsoever in government was gaining traction.

I watched it all through new eyes, wondering aloud if Hillary herself had a good therapist. *Is this what it really means to be a woman?* I wondered with each passing news segment.

The campaign grew darker, more divisive, angrier. Progressive clergy around the country felt our souls stirring in ways we didn't quite know how to deal with. Women rabbis and lawyers and dentists and artists asked themselves if this ugliness only existed within the realm of politics—for shards of it sure felt familiar.

November 8th began with hope, light and pantsuits and ended in tears, panic attacks and a profound sense of fear. And something within me—I would argue, within many of us—came into sharp focus that night. A realization that no matter how detailed our work, how deep our commitment, how intense our love—well, it would never be enough. Whether we aspired to be senior rabbis or chief medical officers or part-time lawyers or stay-at-home supermoms, *it would never be enough.* The social dynamics that had governed our personal and professional worlds since the beginning of time would continue to hold us back until the end of time. And it would never be enough.

And so we took time to heal; we licked our wounds and took deep breaths and attended community gatherings. I preached and prayed and marched and held onto optimism like oxygen, for that's what my therapist advised. I held a congregation in its own morass of anxiety, grief, and fear of what would come. And slowly, steadily, all these different pieces of sadness and loss and empowerment and fierceness and faith all came together to form something new: a different version of the rabbi, wife and mother I'd been all along.

Okay, so maybe "it" would never be enough. But maybe, just maybe, we could change "it," whatever "it" meant to us. Maybe Hillary's defeat was the wake-up call so many of us needed to hear. Maybe we'd taken so much for granted too long. Maybe Hillary's triumph was to sound a battle cry that would echo throughout the generations: every avenue in the world waits, wide open and eager, for *you.*

You just have to forge a new path to get there.

Something shifted in me—I would argue, in most of us, but especially those who identify as women—as we pushed beyond November 8, 2016. The way I moved through the world changed. The way I internalized human stories changed. The way I held congregants in their joy and grief changed. The way I saw the gorgeous, challenging, ancient religion that is Judaism . . . that changed, too.

The most important evolution? The relationship I have with myself. The innate strength I have always possessed—a strength that labeled me "intimidating" from childhood up through my thirties—well, I stopped suppressing it. The apologies I felt I "owed" others for small missteps and misunderstandings? Well, I stopped offering those in abundance. And as for those damn accommodations I offered—*so* often—to men? Slowly but surely, those began to fade into memory.

And I began to focus my energy on raising a feminist son. On building up and empowering women and men surrounding me. On answering misogyny, sexism and racism with love and compassion (as much as I could). On aiming that same love and compassion toward myself. On reading up on my feminist history. On creating the world in which I want to raise *all* children. On normalizing mental illness. On humanizing maternal health.

Maybe this was Hillary's gift: to teach us to fight, not to fear. To love, not to hate. To question, not to assume. To speak up, not shrink back. To seek the fire within each one of us and, once found, let it light the way.

For years I took for granted that which enabled me to pursue my dream of becoming a rabbi. I knew so little about the brave women and men who fought to achieve equality on the pulpit. And for years I misunderstood what it would truly mean to become a mother; the challenges of body, mind, and soul that would form the very spine of my parenthood.

The Hillary Effect, for me? To look toward the rest of my life as a rabbi, a mother and a woman with a renewed sense of purpose, a commitment to equality, and a profound sense of love.

From Fraud to Fighter

Brinda Sarathy

Memory is incomplete and punctuated, highlighting and possibly exaggerating the vicissitudes of our lives so that the past rendered is subjective and fractured. When I think back to my time in graduate school I know that some—if not much of it—must have been exhilarating. Indeed, this was the period during which I met my life companion, conducted arduous fieldwork in the rural Pacific Northwest and forged deep and lasting friendships. Yet, when I think back to my actual schooling experience, I'm mainly left with sentiments of passing trauma and insecurity. I remember feeling like a fraud[1]—like an imposter that somehow made it into the hallowed halls of the flagship UC.

I also know that I did not always feel this way. Indeed, when I first got accepted to UC Berkeley on a scholarship, I was filled with hope and enthusiasm. As an undergraduate, I had been inspired by the likes of Arturo Escobar and Vandana Shiva and was keen on learning and engaging more with the world of international development and its underbelly. And there were certainly others like me in graduate school: bright-eyed, idealistic, intelligent, and optimistic.

Looking back, I can also identify the moments and experiences that marked the slow puncturing of our self-worth, the gradual deflation of our sense of rightful belonging at Berkeley. For me and other graduate student peers, mainly women and people of color, one particular seminar—which I will call "Theory Bros"—was the source of much angst and self-doubt.[2] In that space, what Rebecca Solnit exquisitely identifies as "mansplaining" reigned supreme and many of us were left wondering if we were even visible to the professor and his clique of mostly white, male advisees.[3] The point of Theory Bros seemed to be about tearing down and critiquing all scholarship, and often doing so with an air of mean-spirited performativity that did nothing to foster constructive critique or build a sense of trust or mutual respect. As a result, most women and people of color in the class eventually resigned ourselves to silence, realizing that even when we spoke, our contributions would not be recognized until a white male peer later voiced similar thoughts. Perhaps even more corrosive was that the atmosphere of pervasive criticism led to a general paralysis of writing in the class. We had all become such stellar critics that we could not begin the necessary labor of writing and re-writing constructively, without fear of inner and outer judgment and through the prospect of learning from our mistakes.

Somehow—and largely because we looked out for one another and formed our own networks of mutual support and resilience—my friends and I made it through the violence of Theory Bros and graduate school mostly intact. It took me several more years to shed the feelings of fraudulence and harm perpetuated by that charged environment in which participants felt compelled to outperform one another, whether they actually understood the material or not.

In my academic career today, I am a teacher, researcher, and tenured professor of the liberal arts. Looking back, it is hard not to regard the pomp I witnessed in graduate school (and among some colleagues even today) as stemming from varied insecurities, and to understand their always-talking as, really, a fear of listening. Ultimately, the experience of Theory Bros helped me craft my own teaching to be consciously inclusive, to allow students to be open to learning through failing, and to take risks in order to grow together. Moreover, as a director of a high-profile environmental center and among a handful of women of color academics in a white-dominated field of study, I've used my position and power to diversify and expand understandings of the environment to include conceptions of and action around environmental justice.

This has meant being political and vocal, not shying away from conflict when necessary, and to once again build networks of support and resilience. These networks are especially important in a context where women and people of color have been shown to shoulder a disproportionate amount of service work within academia, whether it is staffing or leading committees, taking notes, getting policies authored, building institutions, informally advising students, and/or doing the follow-up on personnel hires. Gendered service labor is the (often invisible) mortar that keeps institutions cohesive, and it needs to be recognized and justly compensated.

Up until recently, and like many other female colleagues, I was a dependable and competent institutional "work horse." I accepted additional committee responsibilities, stepped up for the benefit of the team and often set aside my own professional research interests for what was ostensibly the greater good. To be clear, no one individual coerced me into taking these decisions. The structural and social conditioning of patriarchy was enough to ensure that women in general would take on roles and responsibilities to ensure the well-being of the larger group or institution, often at personal sacrifice. Over time, then, I found myself taking on more work while also observing how some men who did very little, and did very little not very well, shamelessly took credit for the accomplishments and service of others. I noticed all this, sometimes fumed, but was just too busy working to really process it all.

And then Hillary Clinton lost the election. And something in me snapped into place. I, along with millions of others in the United States of America, bore sorrowful, agonized and dumbfounded witness to the most competent, well-prepared, and qualified candidate in the national race lose to a self-confessed sexual perpetrator and bigot. The stakes for women, children, people of color and immigrants had immediately got a lot higher and continue to remain that way. That moment of loss was another painful reminder of how the progress of so many women and people of color had and have been stymied by heteropatriarchy, and in the case of the US election more specifically, by white male mediocrity.

Hillary's loss helped clarify things in my daily work life. It was not that I was blind to subtle misogyny or the multiple structural forces that help keep women in their place, but I had become numb in some way. Hillary's race, grace and eventual loss shook me out of a stupor of sorts. I suppose anger can help revive in that way. Tangibly, I've been working to encourage and support women to run for city council, and at work I've been advocating for women in leadership positions. I've also lost patience with men who lean on women to do the work for them. I'm more direct about holding people accountable and have no trouble pushing back when needed. It is clear that we need to use our accomplishments for the good of others, to extend a hand down to help other women up, and to not take Hillary's loss in vain, but rather, be inspired by her grit, motivation, and intellect. We not only have a role to play but also are central to being a force for progressive change. Most importantly, we no longer have time to waste fretting over false notions of fraudulence. I'm here to stay and will fight for and build community with others on this journey together.

Part Two

"Agents of Change, Drivers of Progress" Clinton's Role in Shaping Activism

Preface

Denise S. Davis

I'm running because I have a lifetime of experience in getting results and
fighting for people, fighting for kids, for women, for families, fighting to even
the odds, and I know what it takes to get things done.

—Hillary Rodham Clinton

Social movements are rarely credited as being led by women. However, the movement that put "18 million cracks" in the glass ceiling was undeniably led by Hillary Rodham Clinton. Her groundbreaking campaign in 2008 set the stage for igniting a sense of hope and possibility in the 2016 race—from young girls looking for an inspirational figure to emulate, to women in their nineties and beyond who were desperately hanging on to the possibility of seeing the first female president of the United States in their lifetime—Clinton's candidacy ignited a voter base long ignored in American politics. For the first time, female donors made up the majority of contributions (60 percent) to a presidential campaign. People of color and low-income voters overwhelmingly chose Clinton. She garnered 89 percent of all African American voters, 66 percent of all Latino voters, 65 percent of Asian voters and 53 percent of voters with an income of less than $50,000 a year. Zerlina Maxwell, director of progressive media for Clinton's 2016 campaign noted that the "Clinton campaign employed more black women than any other presidential campaign in American history" (Mukhopadhyay and Harding 2017). Her campaigns broke significant barriers to participation in the American political arena. Part 2 highlights the often-overlooked impact that Hillary Clinton and her campaigns have had on initiating movements and creating activists.

Jennifer L. Merolla and Rachel VanSickle-Ward author a chapter entitled "Clinton does inspire," originally published during the 2016 election, which examines the disconnect in the media narrative claiming Clinton lacked enthusiasm surrounding her campaign and the data that proves otherwise. This piece offers an important jumping off point for future activism, as it outlines the media bias that leaves many marginalized voices from being recognized and reflected. As the authors point out, "Claims that Clinton does not inspire are not just inaccurate, they devalue the voices of women of all races and men of color in political discourse."

Contributor to this part and civil rights icon Dolores Huerta notes that where once women thought they had no power, Clinton's run for the highest office is proving to have a catalytic effect on all women—those new to the political stage and also those who have been life-long activists. Paulette Brown-Hinds, publisher and founder of Voice Media Ventures, examines the historical context of the fight for women's rights in the United States, and the dedication to perseverance in the face of setbacks. "Over a century later, that impossibility of failure ignited another generation of women to pick-up the 21st century suffrage banner, but instead of fighting for the right to vote, we were fighting to be on the ballot."

Long-time political operative and activist Torie Osborn details her close connection to the Hillary Clinton campaign in her chapter, "My personal Hillary Effect." Osborn shares stories from high moments of stress on the campaign trail, such as being asked to stand in for Tom Hayden to represent Hillary Clinton on Amy Goodman's "Democracy Now" radio show, and campaigning in swing states, raising money and garnering support during get-out-the-vote efforts (GOTV). Osborn describes her great involvement by saying, "Hillary's campaign jolted my subconscious into action, arming me against rising Trumpism."

Jenn Carson, co-president of the Women's March Inland Empire, discusses how the 2016 election cycle saw the creation of Hillary-inspired private Facebook groups like Pantsuit Nation, which has drawn over four million followers and sixty-five worldwide chapters that continues to communicate and organize. Carson's "State of the Union" on Pantsuit Nation details how the movement lives on, with a focus on how Clinton's candidacy inspired Women's Marches all around the globe. Carson's insider perspective on Pantsuit Nation and the Women's March details the struggles and successes experienced by Hillary Clinton's most dedicated supporters and activists.

Dc Lozano, writer and community activist, poetically captures the impact of the 2016 Presidential Election Day, and what followed in "Glass tumblers." Lozano notes: "The women of the Hillary Clinton Era are exercising their power by engaging in politics in ways never before seen." Her piece is a personal look at how the hope of Hillary's election led to such devastation on Election Night, and how so many women in particular are changed forever as a result.

In "The resistance tips its pussy hat to HRC," Casey B. K. Dominguez, associate professor of Political Science and International Relations, discusses how

Hillary Clinton's candidacy contributed to the massive movement known as the "resistance." Dominguez outlines findings from a small sample which examined how the election impacted people's lives and their participation in activism. Dominguez found that the stereotype portrayed through the media that the #Resistance is fueled by left-leaning Bernie Sanders supporters', is countered by evidence proving that many are in it because they are following Hillary Clinton's lead.

Contributor Shayla Nunnally, associate professor of Political Science, writes in her chapter about the influences that helped shape Clinton's stances on racial justice. Nunnally highlights the impact of the Black Lives Matter movement in the 2016 campaign, and how high-profile and grassroots activism influenced significant shifts in policy, rhetoric and, ultimately, the Democratic Party platform. The Hillary 2016 campaign's national deputy women's vote director, Neisha Blandin, said, "For me, it wasn't just about helping to elect the first woman president, but helping to elect a woman who also centers black women's experiences" (Mukhopadhyay and Harding 2017).

Reference

Mukhopadhyay, S. and K. Harding, ed. (2017), *Nasty Women: Feminism, Resistance, and Revolution in Trump's America*, 1st edn, 219. New York: Picador.

Clinton Does Inspire

The Narrative About Hillary Clinton's "Enthusiasm Gap" Silences the Political Voices of Women

Rachel VanSickle-Ward and Jennifer L. Merolla*

Hillary Clinton was the first woman ever to be nominated to run for president by any major political party in the United States. Despite a formidable challenge from Senator Bernie Sanders, throughout the 2016 primary election, Clinton was significantly ahead in delegates, and acquired more votes than any other candidate in the race from any party—more than 16 million votes in all. While she did not win the general election, she won the popular vote over Donald Trump. Why, then, did journalists and pundits persist in asserting a lack of enthusiasm for Clinton, claiming that she did not inspire during both the presidential primary and general election?

It would be one thing if the data actually supported this narrative. But polling data belies this enthusiasm gap. For example, a Gallup poll of the Democratic primary conducted in late March found that 54 percent of Democrats and Democratic leaners were enthusiastic about Clinton, compared to 44 percent for Bernie Sanders.[1] In 2016 and even into 2017, Clinton was the most admired woman in America, according to Gallup polls (a recognition that she received twenty-two times). There are numerous other examples as well, from young girls awed by Secretary Clinton to older women hoping to see a woman president in their lifetime, to former staffers telling stories that illustrate why they admire her, to critics explaining how she won them over, to the countless images on social media of women wearing suffragette white and/or pantsuits on Election Day in 2016. Indeed, the disconnect between a candidate as widely admired as Clinton

---

* An earlier version of this chapter was first published in US News and World Rerport in June 2016, https://www.usnews.com/opinion/articles/2016-06-02/claims-that-clinton-doesnt-inspire-devalue-womens-political-voices.

and media labeling of her as uninspiring is so stark that the satirical online paper, the Onion, ran a piece with the title "Female Presidential Candidate who was United States Senator, Secretary of State Told to be More Inspiring."

But why did this disconnect emerge in the first place? Part of it is the different ways of measuring enthusiasm. During the primary, pundits would point to large rallies for Sanders as evidence of enthusiasm, but this did not always translate into wins at the ballot box. Clinton's support during the primary and general election largely came from women and people of color, especially women of color (Junn 2017). Given that public advocates for Clinton were often harassed online and even in everyday interactions with others, it is no small wonder that many Clinton supporters felt compelled to do so in secret, for example, via private pro-Clinton Facebook groups such as Pantsuit Nation (see Carson's contribution in this volume). This may in part explain differences in very public expressions of enthusiasm for Sanders or Trump compared to higher enthusiasm for Clinton in polls like Gallup.

More generally, as research by political scientists Christopher Karpowitz and Tali Mendelberg (2014) demonstrates, women's voices are often less amplified in public political discussions. And of course, when women do raise their voices they are frequently accused of shouting.

Another factor cited for the enthusiasm gap was Clinton's high unfavorability ratings. This may have been a genuine vulnerability for Clinton. However, favorability ratings are not measures of enthusiasm or inspiration, and may also be gendered, especially as women seek positions traditionally held by men. As journalist Sady Doyle put it, "America loves women like Hillary Clinton as long as they're not asking for a promotion."[2] Research has long demonstrated that women in leadership roles often face challenges of likeability that male counterparts do not face (Eagly and Karau 2002). When women in leadership roles exhibit traits valued in leaders, such as being assertive, it violates cultural expectations for how women should act, which can in turn lead to lower likeability ratings. The choice of metrics highlighted by the media in spinning this narrative is particularly troubling given the lack of representation of women of all races and men of color in the news media both as journalists and as commentators. As feminist blogger Melissa McEwan argues, enthusiastic support for Clinton "just so happens to be concentrated among populations who are not well-represented among the media influencers primarily responsible for driving this narrative."[3]

It is further important to note that indicators of enthusiasm that were part of the narrative may not capture the ways in which voters may have been enthusiastic about and inspired by Clinton. For example, as later chapters in this volume attest to, Clinton explicitly mainstreamed "women's issues" by centering them in discussions of heath care, economic policy, and gun violence. Women may have therefore been inspired and enthusiastic not just because they saw Clinton as a role model, but because they heard their lives and experiences being talked about in a meaningful way. All the more reason, then, not to discount that enthusiasm.

This is emphatically not to say that all women and people of color were enthusiastic and inspired by Clinton during the 2016 election, or that there weren't men who were also enthusiastic and inspired by her. These groups are not monolithic. Furthermore, not all people who cast a ballot for Clinton were necessarily enthusiastic or inspired by her candidacy.

But the fact is that many of the groups that were most enthusiastic and inspired are those who are least likely to be heard in the public space, because women and people of color are underrepresented in governing and media institutions, and because women are less inclined to express their voices as loudly as men in political spaces. This lack of presence sends a signal that such voices are less important or relevant. So claims that Clinton did not inspire are not just inaccurate; they devalue the voices of women of all races and men of color in political discourse.

References

Eagly, A. H. and S. J. Karau (2002), "Role Incongruity Theory of Prejudice Toward Female Leaders," *Psychological Review*, 109 (3): 573–98.

Junn, J. (2017), "The Trump Majority: White Womanhood and the Making of Female Voters in the U.S.," *Politics, Groups and Identities*, 5 (2): 343–52.

Karpowitz, C. F. and T. Mendelberg (2014), *The Silent Sex: Gender, Deliberation, and Institutions*, Princeton, NJ: Princeton University Press.

8

Dolores Speaks

Hillary's Influence on Activism and Politics

Dolores Huerta and Ivy A. M. Cargile

Dolores Huerta is an activist and feminist who has been fighting for the rights of farmworkers, women and the underrepresented for several decades. Alongside Cesar Chavez she started the United Farm Workers (UFW) union in the Central Valley of California in order to make sure that the rights of farmworkers in the state were protected. It is through her work with the UFW that Huerta met influential women such as Gloria Steinem who inspired Huerta as she embarked on her journey of fighting for women's rights. It is no doubt then that Huerta has been a long-time supporter of Hillary Clinton. During the 2008 election cycle she came out in support of Clinton (as she notes here). As such, in the aftermath of the 2016 presidential election we felt it necessary to speak with her about her views on the candidate and campaign. In 2018, I had the privilege to be in dialogue with her about Clinton and learned the following.

As a labor organizer, immigrant rights activist and feminist advocate Dolores Huerta has worked tirelessly to improve the lives of the poor, women and children. In following her journey, it becomes evident that for her, social justice is not just a goal, but it is a way of life, an approach to existing and living in a society where everyone enjoys equal treatment and protection from harm. It is this sense of duty toward humanity and tending to the needs of others that attracts her to other fellow humanitarians like Hillary Rodham Clinton. For leaders like Huerta and Clinton, life has been about service to others but, in particular, it has been about making sure that women's voices and those of the underrepresented are heard.

In my conversation with Huerta about Clinton's legacy, the image she put forth in describing Hillary was one that looked a lot like a tapestry. A tapestry depicting a life of activism. One where Clinton, from the start, wanted to achieve what many—including her—would consider the impossible. As a young college-aged woman who understood the challenges of gender roles, Clinton believed she could be the catalyst through which some change and equity could be achieved. In part, this fight for women is what intrigued Huerta about Clinton. However, what really caught Huerta's attention was not just her dedication to women but also to migrant farmworkers. We see her commitment to both when Clinton volunteered her time to babysit the children of women migrant farmworkers at the age of eleven in 1956 (Goodwin 2016). This would allow the women to work without worry. Huerta states that when you couple this with her most recent declaration before the United Nations that women's rights are human rights, it is evident that throughout her life—from when she was young through today—she has been on the forefront of the women's rights struggle. It is these instances that remind Huerta of how valuable Clinton has been to the women's rights movement.

She further explains that she is grateful for Clinton's courage to come out strong for women's reproductive rights despite knowing that she would be villainized for this—just as she is maligned for so many other things people dislike about her or what she does.

> I would just say that she probably had people who told her that she should not come out strong for women's reproductive rights because there would be so many people against her—the clergy, other [religious] institutions, and you know the women that are anti-abortion . . . it was a risk for her to do that but she believes in it so the possible enemies didn't matter. She did it anyway.

To hear Huerta describe Clinton's determination on the issue of women's reproductive rights, there is no doubt that Clinton's life as an activist was one full of many battles. Battles that she has fought and continues to fight so that women can have access. Thus, lending a rich piece to that tapestry.

Given Clinton's social justice journey ranging from being a college activist to being active in voter drives, to fighting for universal healthcare, and healthcare for children, her landing on the presidential path is not surprising. To hear Huerta describe it, the United States could have chosen the most qualified, knowledgeable and empathetic candidate for the presidency but due to sexism and misogyny this was thwarted. As Huerta notes, "You know [she was] much more intelligent, knowledgeable . . . everything you know . . . and yet they would elect someone like Donald Trump who does not know [anything]."

In her opinion, Clinton did, however, leave a lasting legacy. For Huerta—as for many others—it is monumental that so many women in the aftermath of Clinton's loss chose to run for political office. This is evidence that while at one point,

> women in our society did not think they had any power . . . not even in their homes . . . things feel different now. I think that even men have been influenced by her run. I think they realized that they have to take the whole issue of women's rights into consideration when they run for office. Women's rights and children's rights have to be included.

This idea that men now have to take women's and children's rights into consideration when running for political office further supports what has already been established, which is that when women run for political office they shed a light on different issues than do male candidates (Anzia and Berry 2011; Smooth 2011; Wittmer and Bouche 2013). There is no doubt that a Hillary Effect has been felt electorally and policy-wise.

Huerta fondly notes that she has had the privilege of encountering and learning about the Hillary Effect for some time now. As she recalls, they first met during Bill's first term as president, when Clinton invited Huerta and other women activists of color to have a "cafecito" at the White House for some input. According to Huerta, she now knows that this was the first of many meetings that she would come to have with Clinton. However, this one in particular was a memorable meeting. She was truly taken aback because as far as she knew no other First Lady had ever asked for the opinions of women activists such as herself.

Huerta recalls:

> She was interested in knowing what our concerns were. She wanted to learn from us what it was that our communities needed so she could take that back to her husband. This was impressive. As a fairly new First Lady she was already thinking about making sure that the new administration would include the policy issues important to Latinas/os and other people of color on the political agenda.

Clinton's inclusivity allows for the political table to be extended to people traditionally left out. This makes it evident to Huerta that Clinton has always sought to hear and understand a diversity of voices.

As time would pass and the paths of these two iconic leaders would continuously cross, it became more apparent why, at one point, Clinton was considered the voice of her generation (Keith 2015). Specifically, she did not shy away from challenges and definitely not from confronting the system on behalf of those who were disempowered. One of the anecdotes that Huerta provides as evidence of this is the path Clinton decided to embark upon after graduating from one of the top Ivy League universities. Huerta notes that upon graduation from Yale, Clinton could have used her degree in a self-serving manner. She could have applied and easily been hired to a prestigious law firm. However, quite the opposite happened in that she chose to work for the Children's Defense Fund as well as take time out to go and register poor Mexicans/Latinas/os to vote in the "colonias of South Texas. She was down there after graduating from Yale. Just her whole history of public service and of not using her law degree from Yale as a kind of platform to promote herself. . . . She is a true example of a public servant." Furthermore, as Huerta explains it, this ethic of hard work that Clinton embodies is what makes her an exceptional leader.

Clinton's past is made up of meaningful experiences that have not only benefited the communities she set out to help but also influenced other legendary women. For Huerta, Clinton represents graciousness and loyalty, but most importantly of all, she embodies progress. In the tapestry that is Clinton's life, as Huerta sees it, every job she has had, and every position she has held (or attempted to hold) has resulted in progress toward access and advancement. As a result, the Hillary Effect will be long-lasting and makes the tapestry of her life so powerful.

References

Anzia, S. F. and C. R. Berry (2011), "The Jackie (and Jill) Robinson Effect: Why Do Congresswomen Outperform Congressmen?" *American Journal of Political Science*, 55 (3): 478–93.

Goodwin, L. (2016), "What Babysitting for Migrant Farmworkers Taught Hillary Clinton About White Privilege," *Yahoo News*, https://www.yahoo.com/news/what-babysitting-for-migrant-farmworkers-1341330999975990.html (accessed December 20, 2018).

Keith, T. (2015), "5 Things You Should Know About Hillary Clinton," *It's All Politics*, https://www.npr.org/sections/itsallpolitics/2015/04/11/395302391/5-things-you should-know-about-hillary-clinton (accessed December 20, 2018).

Smooth, W. (2011), "Standing for Women? Which Women? The Substantive Representation of Women's Interests and the Research Imperative of Intersectionality," *Politics & Gender*, 7 (3): 436–41.

Wittmer, D. E. and V. Bouche (2013), "The Limits of Gendered Leadership: Policy Implications of Female Leadership on Women's Issues," *Politics and Gender*, 9 (3): 245–75.

9

My Personal Hillary Effect

Torie Osborn

Los Angeles, April 2016: I'm hurtling along a dark freeway at 4.22 am, heart pounding with anxiety about the anti-Hillary fervor I'll soon be facing. I'm representing Hillary Clinton in a primary-season debate on Amy Goodman's "Democracy Now" against a well-known local pro-Bernie leftist. My long-time friend, Tom Hayden, asked me to substitute for him; he's sick and unwilling to get up for a 5.00 pm taping. Gulp; okay! (Tom, staunch Hillary supporter, died late that October and was spared the horror of the election.)

Suddenly, a vivid memory pops up. It's 1970, autumn in Middlebury, Vermont. I'm a twenty-year-old, newly transferred college junior, standing with a stranger under a golden maple tree. She thrusts a small piece of paper my way, saying intriguingly: "I'm Barbara and I have a top-secret mission for you." She's a college senior who has quietly organized an "abortion underground" to Montreal, Canada, where it's safe, legal and affordable. She's built a state-wide network of nurses who refer women with unwanted pregnancies to her; she arranges everything and drives them herself to Montreal.

But Barbara is graduating soon and has been looking to pass the torch. I'd arrived a month before and already launched "Notes from Women's Liberation," my weekly column in the campus newspaper. Barbara has found her gal! For decades, I kept that scribbled scrap of paper with the Montreal doctor's contact info—a sacred talisman initiating me into life-long feminist organizing. For the next three years, I work hard keeping Barbara's network active, and driving women to that good doctor a few times a year, in secret acts of civil disobedience until *Roe v. Wade*.

I'd entirely forgotten my encounter under the tree, but forty-six years later, as I walk into a big fight with a "Bernie bro" on TV and radio, I suddenly feel centered and strong and clear. I hold my own that morning, thanks in no small part to the armor generated by my surprise flashback.

That was the first of many intense, sudden memories punctuating the next seven months. The whole experience was especially unlikely because I wasn't a long-loyal Hillary person. In fact, I'd been an ardent Obama supporter in 2008, magnetized in the primary by young people's passion, taking a leave from my position as LA City Deputy Mayor for Antonio Villaraigosa to work as a full-time "super-volunteer" that fall. Obama's campaign even inspired my own first-time political run at age sixty-one for the California State Assembly. (Alas, despite raising $880,000 and an army of young volunteers, I was outgunned by the Sacramento Democratic establishment on behalf of another candidate and lost by 1 percent in the 2012 primary.)

In 2016, I was with Hillary from the start. I listened intently as she gave her Four Freedoms Park speech in April 2015. I'm a loyal Democrat, a long-time lesbian-feminist, born in Denmark, molded by the 1960s—a social-democrat to my bones. So she had to tack left to satisfy me, but, in my sixties, political ideology is not enough. The stakes are ever higher as the brutal far right has systematically overtaken the Republican Party, with their infinite dark money, willingness to lie and contempt for equality. To capture my wholehearted support, you'd better support economic justice, have a solid track record of fighting for human rights *and* be able to get things done: build coalitions, advance ideas, move the levers of power. There was no question in 2016 that my choice was the most accomplished, competent, center-left presidential candidate in American history. And, like me, a feminist shaped forever by the 1960s.

I expected some sexism but was gobsmacked by the barrage of misogyny toward Hillary and her supporters—from the left as well as the right. Now, of course, we know it was enabled by thousands of Russia-funded trolling bots that preyed on divisions among Democrats. Despite those hard-hitting headwinds, I threw myself all-in for Hillary. I couldn't afford to take a leave this time, but I volunteered thirty hours a week, spoke at house parties around LA, organized a weekly phone bank at my home, tweeted and posted daily. I lived for HRC for six months.

I also mobilized folks to travel to Las Vegas to door-knock that last get-out-the-vote week. I'd done the same for Obama in 2008 and 2012, so was astonished at the huge response. My goal was 100 (double 2008) but over 160 showed up! The demographics of "Team T.O." foreshadowed the "Resistance": 70 percent older women, half of whom were new to electoral work. We knocked on 20,000 doors.

After that first flashback in April 2016, vivid dreams and waking memories popped up at least weekly—a steady, almost mystical, connection with my early feminism. I'd be standing at a microphone at a Westside-for-Hillary house-party, and suddenly I was speaking at my first International Women's Day rally in 1971—and a fresh roar would power my Hillary speech. One day, I'd read Hillary's women's health policy online, and that night I'd dream of hammering sheetrock to build the new Vermont Women's Health Center in 1974. In a debate, Hillary would speak out forcefully against gun violence and racism, and I'd flash back to 1982, racing across traffic in NYC to stop a white man with a gun from pummeling a black woman. All were experiences I'd entirely forgotten.

Hillary's campaign jolted my subconscious into action, arming me against rising Trumpism. By the time I arrived in Las Vegas on November 1 for our week of canvassing, I was a feminist Jedi warrior. I also was preternaturally reconnected with my intuition, so I felt deeply uneasy, as though we were battling invisible demons. And, of course, we were. That stark lesson from my early feminism has held true throughout life: my intuition is *always* right.

By Election Night, I knew in my gut the polls were wrong and Hillary couldn't beat back the forces arrayed against her. It was a sad early night for me. But my deepened feminist soul awoke the next day, ready for the struggle ahead. This current civic uprising is for everyone, but it's led by women of all colors—older women like me. Like Hillary.

Team T.O. morphed into "Team TO Resist & Rise," with 125 active members, vibrant monthly meetings and a lead role in the "resistance" network that powered the 2018 California Blue Tsunami. Over three years, we raised $785,000 at five $50 events and canvassed 50,000 doors to help flip two local Congressional seats and an Arizona US Senate Seat. We know our huge army of volunteers, mostly women, is one of thousands rising up across America for democracy, for sanity and humanity. E Pluribus Unum.

As Ruth Bader Ginsberg says, "Time is on the side of change." We represent America's majority on every issue I care about. My resuscitated faith, though sometimes slathered in fury or despair, remains strong—faith in freedom, in the power of ordinary people, in America's promise of "liberty and justice for all." I've seen AIDS decimate my LGBTQ community, only for us then to rise up and gain America's heart and marriage equality in record time. I've seen California transform these past twenty-five years from a conservative, Anglo, anti-immigrant majority to a multicultural, progressive supermajority. When the history of this second American Revolution is written, its story will begin with the tens of thousands of women who, despite the hatred hurled against us, discovered—or rediscovered—our power on the Hillary campaign.

10

Pantsuit Nation

Jenn Carson

In the evening of October 20, 2016, I was invited to join a secret Facebook group created by Libby Chamberlain, a friend of a friend. It was a group of 500 women who planned to wear a pantsuit to the polls to honor Hillary Clinton. As I clicked join, I thought of my paternal grandmother's work on the 1993 Hillary Clinton Health Task Force in Washington, DC, and the 24-year-old anti-Hillary magnet on my Republican mother's refrigerator. When I entered the group, I read the first posts and cried. For the first time in six months, I was in an online space without aggressive male followers of Bernie Sanders or Donald Trump. No one would call me a fat bitch or a snowflake or a libtard.

Within a week, Pantsuit Nation had a million members and formed cultural norms that mirrored the woman we celebrated. There was dignity, compassion and a deep commitment to human rights. There were also celebrations of Women's History, feminism and great female role models like Ida B Wells, Tammy Duckworth and Michelle Obama. Many members who never attended a university were introduced to the concept of intersectionality for the first time. In posts with thousands of comments, there was empathy for the pain expressed in the community. Sexual assault survivors, Latinas, LGBTQIA, the Disabled, black women and others shared their personal fear of Trump's rhetoric. Others posted about shattered relationships with Trump supporting spouses, parents and friends. Some felt unsafe in their church, home, or workplace.

Seemingly overnight, this quiet online gathering of women felt like an antithesis of loud Trump rallies with the pantsuit as a symbolic alternative to the red Make America Great Again hat. Soon I joined the Pantsuit Nation leadership team and formed Pantsuit Nation Inland Empire for members in Inland Southern California. On November 8, 2016, members went to the polls in pantsuits and gathered, prepared to celebrate our first female president. Hillary Clinton even sent Pantsuit Nation a message that read: "Tonight, I hope we'll finally break through that highest, hardest glass ceiling together, and use those pantsuits for the best occasional of all—celebrating." Unfortunately, there would be no celebration that night.

When Hillary lost, Pantsuiters expressed shock, anger, and sadness. How could a vulgar reality star beat the most qualified candidate to ever run for president—a woman who had been a US Senator and Secretary of State? There was also shock that 46 percent of American voters supported the behavior and views of Trump. In Hillary's concession speech, she directly thanked our "secret group" but encouraged members to leave the secret group and take action. She said, "To the millions of volunteers . . . who knocked on doors, talked to neighbors, posted on Facebook—even in secret, private Facebook sites—I want everybody coming out from behind that." In that moment, 4 million members wished they had done more. We had been canvasing, calling voters and posting on Facebook. Should we have been yelling at our own rallies?

The day after the election, a sixty-year-old Pantsuit Nation member in Hawaii, Teresa Shook, posted an event on Facebook called, "I Think We Should March." Her event gained half of a million RSVPs and evolved into a global Women's March of 5 million people worldwide. Women started to leave their homes and hit the streets. Leading up to that march, the Left began to criticize Hillary Clinton, Hillary supporters, and Pantsuit Nation for not doing enough to win. Members of color rightfully also called out Pantsuit Nation as a place for white women to hide behind computers and feel "woke." Libby Chamberlain, the founder of Pantsuit Nation was also panned for turning the grief of her millions of members into a coffee table book. This backlash resulted in think pieces, mostly by men, with titles like, "Pantsuit Nation is a Sham." The criticism of Pantsuit Nation and Hillary Clinton contained equal parts valid critique and misogyny. When Pantsuit Nation, Hillary Clinton, and Teresa Shook were not featured in the Women's March, the shift was complete. We were no longer focused on Hillary Clinton. We were now uniting around the world to fight bigotry. We were forming an intersectional movement to promote human rights and progressive democratic values. The moment of the US presidential election had triggered a global movement against neo-nationalism.

As we approach the four-year anniversary of the loss of Hillary Clinton, I'll offer a brief State of the Union for Pantsuit Nation (now merged with Supermajority). We have evolved into a group of 4 million diverse members and we are now led by Cortney Tunis, an executive director who is a brilliant woman of color and a woman of action. We have over sixty-five chapters around the world including my chapter, Pantsuit Nation Inland Empire which has 750 members in Inland Southern California. In both our local chapter and the national group, we still get personal about how the Trump era impacts us directly but we are primarily focused on amplifying and engaging in action related to protecting human rights and electing Democratic candidates—especially candidates who are women, people of color, Muslim, LGBTQIA, and other underrepresented groups. Also, while I remain a Pantsuit Nation leader, much of my own personal work is done through established groups like my local Democratic Club and other grassroots organizations like Women's March California. The same is true of my local members who spend every weekend involved in civil action, community-organizing, and peaceful protest.

Are the members of Pantsuit Nation just lazy latte liberals who sit behind computers at Starbucks? Yes, some are—but the majority have taken Hillary Clinton's call to action. We are doing the painstaking process of confronting our privilege and amplifying marginalized voices. Are we great activists? No. We are beginning activists. Pantsuit Nation was initially a movement lacking movement. As we move forward, we must accept Hillary's call to action. Pantsuiters must recognize that many of the fears expressed in Pantsuit Nation in October 2016 have come true in 2019. President Trump has attacked women, people of color, LGBTQIA, Muslims and, worse, caged immigrant toddlers and children. Like Hillary Clinton in her 11th hour of congressional testimony in 2015, we must not take a break or give up. We must fight for human rights, fight for democracy, and fight our instinct to hide at home—inside a secret online group.

11

Glass Tumblers

Dc Lozano

The thin horizon of a plan is almost clear, my friends and I have had a
tough time, bruising our brains hard up against change.

—*The Wood Song, Indigo Girls*

In the months leading up to the 2016 presidential election, and the ensuing eons after, ephemera of the glory days of male chauvinism inundated our lives. Crooked Hillary became a jingoistic chant, an opiate for the asses. A "Repeal the 19th" hashtag took flight. Locker room banter became an excuse to grab PC by the standards and call them attacks on freedom of speech. Lock Her Up was hollered so many times I googled if Tourette's syndrome could be caused by mass hysteria.

We'd been Trump-ed. Our clocks turned back. It was Bro-light Savings Time. Instead of the Hillary Clinton Epoch launching us ahead, our forward momentum was flipped upside down, held by its feet over a cavern of yore, and shaken until every gain we'd made was chipped, smudged, distorted, or lost completely; our hopeful pockets emptied of all our Nasty Woman buttons and I'm With Her enamel pins. As each day passed, more and more people filed Missing Country reports. It was as though the Cliff's Edge of Insanity had appeared overnight like aliens in our beautiful blue sky. The truth was, though, that someone had just pulled the horizon-colored backdrop down and exposed the real America behind it.

Fake news, fake crimes, fake accounts. The focus of the media was like that of toddlers trying to sit at the adult table at Thanksgiving. They peered over the top of the table on their tip toes taking the scraps they were given by the biggest turkey in history. Instead of talking about candidate platforms and how those candidates planned to enact those platforms, the toddlers took their scraps like the hidden side-show at a side-show—the one in the back that you had to pay extra to see because what was in that tent was something never seen by humanity before. The media spent less than 10 percent of their time covering actual politics and policy, while they repeated or aired Lock Her Up and Emails! They led the way down the red brick road, ignoring every warning sign, even the ones they uttered aloud. They expressed constant dismay: how can he say these things they said, as they said the thing he said again and again. The dog became the underdog became the leader of a rabid pack of mongrels.

I ran an extra mile on Election Day. I told myself if I pushed those extra 5,280 feet, Hillary would be certain to win. I told myself that any discomfort I endured would mean that the invocation of my feet pounding on the pavement, the drumming of my heart and the rhythm of my breath would call out to the universe a prayer surely to be answered with the Ultimate Feminist Trophy. We find ways, don't we, to bargain with the universe. This was my bargain: one mile more for every time some dude called me a feminazi or a dyke, a cunt, or a whore. One mile more for God Damn It We Deserve This. One mile more for President Hillary Rodham Clinton. I thought One Mile More would be enough. I swore to every possible goddess that I would run that mile in bare feet, over glass ceiling splinters, on the anniversary of her election—For The Rest Of My Life—if it meant my blood oath would be accepted. I guess the universe, in all her wisdom, knew it didn't need a female POTUS to collect my suffering.

Maybe it's the purposefully planted bias embedded in the walls of my psyche that allows me to believe that my suffering is what will bring me success—that literal blood, sweat, and tears are my only bargaining chips. Maybe it's as tiring to the universe as it was to Hillary; as it has been for me, for women everywhere. Maybe the universe, the mothering spirit of our existence, seeks to allay this deeply rooted belief, instead, with the soothing assurance of liberation. That all she wants is a promise, finally, that we will love our bodies, our voices, our minds. To love the her in each of us, in all the varieties she can be. Maybe she too is exhausted by the paradigm that measures the value of women by a scale used to exploit our threshold of pain. Maybe she's saying that I'm With Her, isn't just about being with Hillary, it's about being with a her universal, it's about negating the idea that women are second-class citizens; maybe it's a demand that I'm With Her means believing, once and for all, that I'm With Me, too.

In 2013, the Obama administration ended the Presidential Physical Fitness Test as we know it. As those who endured the humiliation of standardized failure in front of our classmates can attest, its cessation was long overdue. Was it possible, though, that it was the worst jinx in history? Is it mere coincidence that without this yearly Ode to Angst, we lost our ability to burn off unsightly baggage, both literal and figurative? I know that literally my figure has gone up at least a size since my own 45—and you know the White House gets it. Look at the weight it took on at the same number.

Voter turnout went from growth to girth as civic metabolism also slowed. We came to on November 9, 2016 weighted, facing the workout plan nobody expected. The get in shape Right Freaking Now plan. The Zero HRC Core & Cardio Life/Body Fitness program brought to you by a lack of proper consumption at the Dining Table of Civic Responsibility—an abstention from the American dream, from sustenance for all, replaced, instead, with one too many White Russians imbibed by those unable to handle their fodder and feed. I mean, what body politic can stomach three parts heavy cream in anything knocked back by the millions—in, of all things, an Old-Fashioned glass.

But that old tumbler can be smashed like any outmoded mug, replaced with something that will actually help a little, a Chardonnay, maybe, and a long walk in the woods. The Day After felt like the world had a chalk outline around it. I knew my survival meant hitting my own I'm With Her Gym as hard and as often as possible, doing the arduous work of getting in the kind of shape that will allow me to suffer less and support more. The women of the Hillary Clinton era are exercising their power by engaging in politics in ways never before seen on this sea to shining sea. We gained something from Hillary, from watching her relentless ability to stay standing and fight back, that they will never again be able to put asunder. So, as we move toward dismantling the system that has held firm our chains, I ask you to make this bargain with the universe instead: that we forevermore deny that our success must come with pain and starvation.

We'd bumped our knees on a broken edge of the American dream. You can rub it until the pain goes away, but there's a little broken bell of it that still rings through you every time a woman's right to choose in another state is limited or taken away, every time another black body is gunned down by police, every time someone says fag or homo, every trans woman that is found dead in the streets and identified by the media as a man in a dress, every time someone guns down children or concert-goers.

We will never forget that we were devastated that night. That we broke like glass. That we fell to the ground and raised our waterlogged fists, salty in defiance, as we wiped away our tears. We shattered that evening. Because we are the glass ceiling. We, like the shrapnel of an exploding sun, are everywhere now reflecting *her*. We are a million prisms lighting the way out of the patriarchy, and we will have an Oval Office of our own.

12

Failure Is Impossible

Paulette Brown-Hinds

The moment I learned of Hillary Clinton's loss for her historic bid for the presidency of the United States, my universe shifted. And like more than half the nation, and I suspect most of the rest of the world, I felt like I woke up in a strange place. A place where walls replaced bridges, division defeated unity, hate trumped love and where "surreal" was the dominant state of mind simply because so many of us just couldn't believe what was happening. We hadn't just failed to elect the first female president, we failed to uphold the values of this country, the values so many of us fight to maintain every day, important values our ancestors sacrificed their lives to protect: unity, equality, diversity.

Every summer I make a pilgrimage to sacred ground, the home of Susan B. Anthony, a national historic landmark in Rochester, New York. It's the place where she lived while leading efforts in both the suffrage and abolition movements and where she was arrested in 1872 in her living room for daring, as a woman, to exercise the right to vote. She was a woman who devoted her life to the fight for equality—for women and African Americans. And while women were not granted the right to vote during her lifetime, she clearly knew that eventually someday we would win our fight for the franchise. At a birthday celebration in Washington, DC, a few weeks before her death, she told well-wishers, "There have been others also just as true and devoted to the cause—I wish I could name everyone—but with such women consecrating their lives, failure is impossible" (Sherr, 1995).

Her three final public words, "failure is impossible" became the motto for the suffrage movement and the ongoing fight for women's rights. Those words, journalist Lynn Sherr called "the keynote" of Ms Anthony's life and "the slogan under which an army of women" would eventually march to victory (Sherr, 1995).

Over a century later, that impossibility of failure ignited another generation of women to pick-up the twenty-first-century suffrage banner, but instead of fighting for the right to vote, we were fighting to be on the ballot. Chasing Hillary, author Amy Chozick captured the sentiment in a *New York Times* article: "The role she played in spurring a wave of activism has become more clear. By losing," she noted, Hillary "set-off a national awakening among women . . . prompting women's marches" and "a record number of female candidates running for office" (Chozick 2018).

Women marched because they were inspired by Hillary's service. Women marched because they were angry. And women marched because they were ready to fight back . . . And fight back they did. Not only did women march in small cities, diverse metros and communities across the globe, but they also committed to pick up where Hillary left off. By the midterm elections, record numbers of women ran for both the House of Representatives and the United States Senate. More women were nominated for governor, and there were more women—diverse and younger women—serving in the House. Hillary was known to have once said to her classmates, "Practice politics as the art of making what appears to be impossible, possible" (Rodham Clinton 1969). Viewed through a different lens, Hillary's failure to win the presidency was the spark that led to a renewed passion for equal rights, including the right to serve the public. Hillary may have lost the presidency but—from the halls of Congress to local city halls across America—more women started running for office and more women won.

Hillary is now part of a select club of presidential candidates whose defeat led to larger cultural movements, historian Doris Kearns Goodwin noted, "It's hard to see when you're in the middle of it. But it feels like something's happening, a fervor, an excitement, an optimism" (Chozick 2018). In a birthday letter sent to Ms Anthony by her colleague Mary Howell before her death, she wrote: "You will be a great light on the world's highway for the coming centuries" (Harper 1908). It may have taken fourteen years after Ms Anthony uttered her famous last public words before the 19th Amendment giving women the right to vote was signed into law, but her light was not extinguished even with her death.

Over a century later those three words "failure is impossible" still inspire us and remind those of us devoted to the cause and the continued fight for equality that every setback and every loss contains the opportunity for success.

References

Chozick, A. (2018), "Hillary Clinton Ignited a Feminist Movement by Losing," *The New York Times*, January 13.

Harper, I. H. (1908), *The Life and Work of Susan B. Anthony*, Indianapolis: The Hollenbeck Press.

Rodham Clinton, H. (1969), "Commencement Speech," Wellesley College, Wellesley, MA.

Sherr, L. (1995), *Failure Is Impossible: Susan B. Anthony in Her Own Words*, New York: Random House.

The #Resistance Tips Its Pussy Hat to HRC

Casey B. K. Dominguez

When Hillary Rodham Clinton lost the presidency to Donald Trump, one of the major consequences was to propel millions of Americans into the streets in protest. College-educated Democratic women had an especially visceral reaction against Trump, exemplified by the thousands of women who marched in the 2017 Women's March wearing hand-knitted hot pink "pussy hats," an obvious reference to Trump's remarks on the infamous Access Hollywood tape. The Women's March and its organizers (and Donald Trump and his policies) certainly deserve credit for empowering the #Resistance.[1] But Hillary Clinton's historic candidacy also had an impact on the movement that arose after her loss.

If you scratch the surface of the organized anti-Trump political universe, you find a great deal of respect, and some outright love, for Hillary Rodham Clinton. Though hard data is still scarce, some evidence suggests that the #Resistance is significantly populated by women, especially older Democratic women.[2] That is a demographic that during 2016 contained a large number of enthusiastic Hillary supporters.[3] From October to December 2016, more than 3 million people, predominantly women, joined a secret Facebook group that also served as a nucleus of #Resistance organizing. The group, Pantsuit Nation, was a Clinton fan club named after Hillary Clinton's "Sisterhood of the Traveling Pantsuits."[4] After the election, Pantsuit Nation itself became apolitical, but other Facebook groups became political offshoots of the group. One of the largest is Together We Will, with 400,000 members. An uncountable number of other small, local, secret spinoffs remain active today.

In a small sample of mostly female #Resistance members in one blue city,[5] respondents report that their lives have been turned upside down since 2016. They report attending multiple marches and protests, contacting their elected officials, making calls, and knocking on doors for local Democratic candidates, giving money to candidates and established progressive groups, and meeting regularly with new friends and acquaintances in a variety of locally organized #Resistance groups. For all, these activities mark a dramatic change from their lives before 2016. A few had protested "in the '60s," a few had attended party meetings or given money before, but most reported that voting was their only regular political activity prior to the 2016 election.

Though media reports sometimes suggest that the #Resistance is composed of left-leaning Bernie Sanders supporters, other evidence suggests the #Resistance is following Hillary Clinton's example rather than Sanders'.[6] In my small sample of new activists, nearly all had voted for Hillary Clinton in the 2016 general election.[7] Seventy percent had supported Hillary Clinton in the primary as well. The few Bernie supporters in the #Resistance, at least in this sample, were not interested in re-litigating the primary. About half said they just supported Clinton because they always voted for Democrats, but even they were not overly critical. One said, "I think people are way more harsh on her than they should be; I think she is too corporate but not bad enough not to vote for her." Another said, the Democrats "underestimated that sense of hatred and the lies and misinformation that had been spread around way before the election. They ran the worst possible candidate due to that. But Hillary herself was extremely well qualified and well deserving to be president." Other, larger studies of #Resistance activists will have to see whether these sentiments are representative of new activists as a whole. But at least in one highly activated suburban community, the #Resistance is comprised of more Clinton fans than haters.

Of the larger number of activists who supported Hillary Clinton in the 2016 primary, 72 percent had at least one very positive thing to say about her, most frequently mentioning that they felt she was "qualified," "experienced," "intelligent," and that she would have be a "good president." Serious Clinton fans are also easily found. A few had worked on her campaign or had read her books and gone to book signings. A quarter of those who supported her in the primary proudly volunteered that they "liked," "loved" or "admired" her. One said Hillary Clinton was "my life-long hero," and that "I felt like her loss was our country's loss and I felt like we were obligated to pick up what she wasn't able to carry forward." Another woman who said she "admired" Hillary said that "I saw myself in her and other women I respect in her, being able to keep a cool head when under a lot of pressure."

Tellingly, many respondents, when asked about their feelings about Hillary Clinton, felt the need to defensively contrast their support for her with an explanation for why "other people" hate her so much. As one woman put it,

I'm an empathetic person but I have a really hard time seeing the other side of it. She has served so many positions in government—Secretary of State, Senator, she is knowledgeable about policy and how to create policy that is good for the American people, she stood up to every confrontation, to compare the two of them and put him above her is mind boggling.

The new activists who spoke to me readily referred to Clinton's womanhood and to the sexism they felt she was subjected to as part of her campaign. One said that, "I feel like because she's a woman she was judged much more harshly than any man would have been. She has the political experience to have been a great president. Every candidate has their flaws and it was taken to another level because of misogyny." Another said that "I'm almost 50, I've experienced a millionth of what she's experienced in terms of condescension and misogyny, she's got incredibly thick skin; I think she's brilliant, amazing."

When I asked these new political activists what motivates them to immerse themselves in local activism for the first time, they talk about Trump's threats to democracy, racism and xenophobia, and to a lesser degree other core Democratic policy issues like reproductive rights, health care, and the environment. They don't refer explicitly to Hillary Clinton or her campaign. But the example she set, the respect she earned and the unfair treatment she received at the hands of the media and the man who became president stand tall in the background of the Trump #Resistance and are a testament to her service.

References

Clinton, H. (2008), "Speech to the Democratic National Convention," August 26, https://www.npr.org/templates/story/story.php?storyId=94003143.

Fisher, D. (2018), "Here's Who Actually Attended the March for Our Lives. (No, It Wasn't Mostly Young People)," *The Washington Post/Monkey Cage Blog*, March 28. LA Kaufman.

VanSickle-Ward, R. and J. L. Merolla (2016), "Clinton Does Inspire," *US News and World Report*, June 2.

Weigel, D. (2018), "Democratic Party's Liberal Insurgency Hits a Wall in Midwest Primaries," *Washington Post*, August 8.

14

The Hillary (Counterfactual) Effect

A Peculiar Paradox of Policy History and the Influence of Black Political Activism

Shayla C. Nunnally

Hillary Clinton ran for the 2016 presidential candidacy with political experiences unlike any of the other candidates running for the office. A former First Lady, US Senator, and US Secretary of State, Hillary's dossier offered an impressive background in receiving and interacting with public officials and heads of state, serving constituents, representing the nation's interests internationally, and declaring policy stances in state, national, and international contexts. However, it is also Hillary's policy stances as a former First Lady that became her political bane.

It is here that I depart from some of the more positive acclaims of Hillary's 2016 presidential bid effects, in order to discuss the sobering political paradox that her candidacy presented for black politics—what might be considered political negatives for the Hillary campaign that turned into a political positive for the black political agenda. While Clinton appeared to have support among black political elites (e.g., Congress members and traditional, civil rights organizations), younger, progressive black political activists and scholars (e.g., Black Lives Matter and Michelle Alexander) openly and publicly questioned her (and, former president Bill Clinton) on the campaign trail and on social media (activists' tweets on Twitter; Vonk 2017) about her political legacy and its negative effect on the quality of American black life. It is through this contestation that we see an eventual reformation in Clinton's adoption of racial justice policy expand to her candidate platform and the platform of the Democratic Party.

Since 1964, partisan polarization has been racialized (Carmines and Stimson 1989; Drutman 2016), with black voters becoming mostly Democrats and (Southern) white voters realigning from being Democrats to Republicans (Pew Research Center 2012, 2018). It is here that party politics have created an "electoral trap," as Frymer (1999) submits, leaving black voters without much partisan choice beyond the Democratic Party, because the Republican Party has decidedly built outreach with white voters by employing race-baiting strategies (Mendelberg 2001) that distance black voters (Fauntroy 2007). The Democratic Party, also interested in retaining white moderate voters, has played the "race card" through building political campaigns based on racialized policy issues like crime and welfare that function as implicit racial appeals (Mendelberg 2001). Not only have these policies ignored the interests and needs of black Americans, but they have also resulted in anti-black and racially punitive policies against people of color, and black (women) people, in particular (Alexander 2012; Hancock 2004).

The use of these strategies taints the political record of former, Democratic Party presidential candidates, Hillary and Bill Clinton, who similarly used them to gain white electoral support. As legal scholar Michelle Alexander (2016) writes, "From the crime bill to welfare reform, policies Bill Clinton enacted—and Hillary Clinton supported—decimated black America." For example, the 1994 Violent Control and Law Enforcement Act led to massive increases in black Americans' incarceration rates due to disproportionate sentencing in illegal drug offences (Alexander 2016). The Personal Responsibility and Work Opportunity Reconciliation Act of 1996, which Clinton signed into law to "end welfare as we know it," led to a doubling in extreme poverty levels. While much of Alexander's critique focuses on President Clinton, she explicitly notes that First Lady Hillary Clinton was more active in policy pronouncements than other first ladies had been and claims that Hillary, therefore, also "owns" the effects of her husband, President Clinton's actions. For example, in 1996, Hillary delivered a speech in New Hampshire in support of President Clinton's 1994 Violent Crime Control and Law Enforcement Act (*Newsweek* Staff 2017).

Against this backdrop, Black Lives Matter, as a movement, sought to change how black people fit onto the Democratic Party agenda—no longer as social pariahs (as implicitly, party-ascribed, "undeserving members of society") but as invaluable change agents and unapologetically, meaningful voters of the Democratic Party. They did this by directly confronting Clinton on the campaign trail. For example, it was Hillary's infamous quote about the need to be "tough on crime" that Black Lives Matter activist, Daunasia Yancey, confronted Hillary at a New Hampshire political rally to qualify and recant her statement, "They are not just gangs of kids anymore. They are often the kinds of kids that are called 'super-predators.' . . . We can talk about why they ended up that way, but first we have to bring them to heel."

As historian, Donna Murch (2016), contends, Yancey forced Hillary to accept her role in the race-targeted War on Drugs, stating,

> You and your family have been personally and politically responsible for policies that have caused health and human services disasters in impoverished communities of color through the domestic and international War on Drugs that you championed as First Lady, Senator, and Secretary of State. And, so I just want to know how you feel about your role in that violence, and how do you plan to reverse it?

Murch, furthermore, argues that Yancey also forced Hillary to accept her own personal responsibility in creating these destructive measures.

Hillary and Bill have, since, acknowledged their role in these policies and have recognized their damaging effects. Black Lives Matter activists also called on former Secretary of State Hillary Clinton and Senator Bernie Sanders, both Democratic Party leading contenders for the 2016 presidential race, to acknowledge "Black Lives Matter," by asking about criminal justice issues and police-related killings (Lind 2015). Saying this signaled a focal point—addressing issues specific to Black Americans—that, arguably, the Democratic Party has long attempted to refuse to accept in its attempt to redirect the party toward white, moderate voters, whom it has continued to lose as supporters since its national assumption of advancing civil rights in the interest of redressing racial discrimination against black Americans (and other groups) since the 1960s.

It is in Hillary's candidacy as the eventual party nominee that we see the Democratic Party platform expanded to include policy proclamations that, theretofore, were less visible on the party's agenda—attention to *racial* justice and criminal justice issues specific to the experiences of black Americans. This was despite a five-decades-long relationship of overwhelming black support for the Democratic Party at levels of partisan subscription that reached almost 90 percent of black voters. Rather, in the controversies that surrounded Hillary's relationships with race-related issues such as mass incarceration and police-related shootings and killings, her mere presence as a candidate (with such a complex, political record on race-related issues) led to a targeted response of black activists challenging her past and changing the context of political debate, moving the Democratic Party more "leftward." Recognizing Hillary's presence in this does not occlude recognizing the agency of young, black activists who challenged her political past.

It is in the activism of Black Lives Matter activists that we also see Hillary's provocation to be publicly responsive and responsible for acknowledging the plight of black Americans in the criminal justice system—whether as incarcerated persons or targets of racial violence encapsulated in police-related shootings and killings. In Hillary's own words about criminal justice, "Everyone should have respect for the law and be respected by the law" (McCammon 2016). In her own view, since the 2016 presidential election, Hillary (2017) also argues that the Trump administration has cast the United States into a "crisis of democracy"; one such grievance being that President Donald J. Trump disrupts national unity with hate speech. Moreover, she charges the Republican Party with complicity in this polarization and even disfranchisement of black Americans, although citing the Republican Party as having done such political maneuvers much further in advance than the racialized political emergence of the Trump presidency.

Hillary's historic 2016 presidential run (and Senator Bernie Sanders') created the opportune moment for the Black Lives Matter movement and young, progressive activists to re-calibrate the foci of the Democratic Party to include openly the farther-left agenda of racial justice issues: they accomplished this, effectively. The political environment was ripe for any candidate (just like Sanders) to be challenged equally about racial issues specific to black Americans. However, the counterfactual of whether the extent of movement in the Democratic Party's leftward shift would have been what it was without the complicated past of Hillary Clinton will be unknown, as far as whether it would have been possible without Hillary's candidacy.

Without Hillary addressing these issues the party stood to open an even greater gaping hole in its ability to appeal to (especially, younger) black voters post-Obama.[1] It is this same paradox of addressing black political issues and race and politics that will determine the relevance, political stability and electoral success of the Democratic Party in 2020. Indeed, Hillary's effect seems obvious today, as, to date, several Democratic Party candidates, who have declared their presidential candidacies, have been open about their stances on reparations for past injustices committed against black Americans. It also seems apparent in the Trump era, wherein race and politics has explicit consequences for certain groups, that the party and its candidates stand to lose swaths of voters of color, if they do not have the courageous will to listen, incorporate and propose actions on race-related policy issues.

References

Alexander, M. (2012), *The New Jim Crow: Mass Incarceration in the Age of Colorblindness*, New York: The New Press.

Alexander, M. (2016), "Why Hillary Clinton Doesn't Deserve the Black Vote," February 10, https://www.thenation.com/article/hillary-clinton-does-not-deserve-black-peoples-votes/ (December 4, 2018).

Carmines, E. G. and J. A. Stimson (1989), *Issue Evolution: Race and the Transformation of American Politics*, Princeton, NJ: Princeton University Press.

Clinton, H. R. (2017), "American Democracy Is in Crisis," *The Atlantic*, September 16, https://www.theatlantic.com/ideas/archive/2018/09/american-democracy-is-in-crisis/570394/ (December 4, 2018).

Drutman, L. (2016), "How Race and Identity Became the Central Dividing Line in American Politics," *Vox*, August 30, https://www.vox.com/polyarchy/2016/8/30/12697920/race-dividing-american-politics (December 4, 2018).

Fauntroy, M. K. (2007), *Republicans and the Black Vote*, Boulder, CO: Lynne Rienner Publishers.

Frymer, P. (1999), *Uneasy Alliances: Race and Party Competition in America*, Princeton, NJ: Princeton University Press.

Hancock, A. (2004), *The Politics of Disgust: The Public Identity of the Welfare Queen*, New York: New York University Press.

Lind, D. (2015), "Black Lives Matter v. Bernie Sanders, Explained," August 11, https://www.vox.com/2015/8/11/9127653/bernie-sanders-black-lives-matter (December 8, 2018).

McCammon, S. (2016), "Between Police and Black Lives Matter, Hillary Clinton Walking a Fine Line," *NPR*, August 19, https://www.npr.org/2016/08/19/490622277/between-police-and-black-lives-matter-hillary-clinton-walking-a-fine-line (December 8, 2018).

Mendelberg, T. (2001), *The Race Card: Campaign Strategy, Implicit Messages, and the Norm of Equality*, Princeton, NJ: Princeton University Press.

Murch, D. (2016), "The Clintons' War on Drugs: When Black Lives Didn't Matter," *The New Republic*, February 9, https://newrepublic.com/article/129433/clintons-war-drugs-black-lives-didnt-matter (December 4, 2018).

Newsweek Staff (2017), "Twitter Erupts Over News That Hillary Clinton Used Black Prison Labor While First Lady of Arkansas," June 7, https://www.newsweek.com/hillary-clinton-prison-labor-african-americans-arkansas-622209 (December 4, 2018).

Pew Research Center (2012), "A Closer Look at the Parties in 2012," August 23, http://www.people-press.org/2012/08/23/a-closer-look-at-the-parties-in-2012 (December 8, 2018).

Pew Research Center (2018), "An Examination of the 2016 Electorate, Based on Validated Voters," August 9, http://www.people-press.org/2018/08/09/an-examination-of-the-2016-electorate-based-on-validated-voters/ (December 8, 2018).

Vonk, E. (2017), "The Impact of Black Lives Matter on Hillary Clinton's Message on Racial Justice," *Diggit Magazine*, October 11, https://www.diggitmagazine.com/papers/impact-black-lives-matter-hillary-clinton-s-message-racial-justice (December 7, 2018).

Appendix Table 1 OLS Model of Black Americans' Feeling Thermometer about Hillary Clinton

	Coefficients	S.E.
Second World War Generation (Born Before 1941)	14.74	24.09
Civil Rights Generation (Born 1941–1953)	21.56***	6.956
Mid-Civil Rights Generation (Born 1954–1964)	11.37**	5.647
Post-Civil Rights Generation (Born 1965–1981)	3.746	5.570
Female	-1.247	4.177
Education	0.8491	1.518
Registered Voters	-11.41	7.438
Party (Democrats)	35.74****	5.101
Police Force against Black Americans More Than Necessary	-0.0177	2.416
Discrimination Against Black Americans	-0.2375	2.187
Constant	50.42****	12.58

Source: 2016 ANES Pilot Study

Note: Unweighted sample; n = 133; *p≤.10; **p≤.05; ***p≤.01; ****p≤.001; Feeling Thermometer about Hillary Clinton (0 = Cold to 100 = Warm); Generations are compared to Black millennials (born after 1981); "Party" represents a comparison of Democrats to Republicans

Part Three

"When There Are No Ceilings, the Sky's the Limit": Clinton's Impact on Campaigns and Elections

Preface

Ivy A. M. Cargile

I am not a natural politician, in case you haven't noticed . . . unlike my husband or President Obama . . . I have to do the best that I can.

—Hillary Clinton[1]

Hillary Clinton's remark may strike some as surprising, especially since she has been a successful politician for decades. However, these types of sentiments are often heard in studies that look at political ambition among women (Fox & Lawless, 2011; Crowder-Meyer, 2013). Women feel the need to be even more qualified than men when they throw their hat in the electoral arena (Anzia & Berry, 2011; Lazarus & Steigerwalt, 2018). This intuition makes sense given that women candidates are not perceived as leaders (Johnson, et al. 2006; Bauer, 2018). In order to appear as leaders, they often emphasize more masculine qualities (Eagly, et al. 1992; Bauer, 2018), which sometimes puts them in a bind of being perceived as leaders, but not as well liked. Furthermore, women are tasked with navigating a gendered terrain in elections (Hawkesworth, 2003; Dittmar, 2015). As Clinton's experiences have demonstrated, while the terrain is full of challenges, there are also opportunities, and many were left inspired by Clinton's historic run.

In Part 3, we focus on the electoral impact of Hillary Clinton. There are three key effects that the contributors touch on here. First, a number of works discuss the campaign, and how Clinton navigated the challenging terrain faced by women running for office. Second, another set of scholars discuss lessons from Clinton's campaign on appealing to diverse electorates in meaningful ways. A final set of contributions examines the effect of Clinton in the aftermath of the election, both as a role model and in sparking important conversations.

Turning first to campaign effects, Clinton's historic run for the presidency builds on the existing scholarship noted earlier and provides further evidence of what works and what does not work for strong, qualified women candidates seeking high levels of office. Due to the experiences that Clinton had on the campaign trail, women running for office have a somewhat clearer idea about how to present themselves, and how to present the skills and qualifications they bring to the table. In 2016, we observed that sexism and gender stereotypes are still tremendous obstacles for women running for executive office (Jalazai, 2018). Clinton's run provided a better understanding about how gender stereotypes function at the presidential level. However, Hillary also showcased how these dynamics can be improved. The group of women candidates who sought the Democratic nomination for the presidency in 2020 had the benefit of having Clinton's experience to guide them and make them stronger candidates— something she was not afforded. The contributions in Part 3 speak to both the challenges and the opportunities that Clinton faced on the campaign trail.

Specifically, Carrie Skulley questions when women who want to lead will not be plagued by hostility and negative characterizations. In this entry aptly titled, "Hillary Clinton: The exception and the rule," Skulley describes how Clinton's political life story should serve as a cautionary tale that proves that people are more willing to consume stories about her being "powerhungry," and "narcissistic" than to listen to her explain her policy positions. Thus, even if women are as likely to be successful when they choose to run for office as men (Herrnson, et al. 2003; Dolan, 2014), the sexism and hostility women face on the campaign trail is still alive and well.

However, Clinton was able to overcome some of the hurdles that Democratic women often face when running for office, especially at the executive level. Holman, Merolla, and Zechmeister discuss why women competing for executive office are at a disadvantage when people are concerned with national security issues. They then turn to ways in which Clinton was able to combat gender stereotypes from her path as a senator for New York to her position as Secretary of State. According to their analysis, it was Clinton's cultivation of expertise in national security issues that ameliorated peoples' skepticism around having a woman in a position of power during times of elevated terror threats.

The other contributors speak to how Clinton was able to shift understandings of political leaders, by also highlighting feminine strengths. Kelly Dittmar depicts the importance of embracing womanhood in political campaigns. In "Rethinking gender as an electoral asset," Dittmar recounts how Clinton's campaign staff in 2008 wanted to craft an image of her that did not emphasize her gender, thus making it the elephant in the room. She discusses how this approach did not work, and how the re-crafted image of Clinton in 2016 as a candidate who celebrated her gender won people over. While many previous campaigns of women politicians have shown that female candidates will do what they can to portray a masculinized image (Larson, 2001), for Clinton in 2016, this was upended. In an advantageous campaign move, Clinton embraced being a woman and her gender became one of her biggest assets.

Another asset that being a woman bestowed upon Clinton was that of motherhood. Greenlee and VanSickle-Ward discuss how Clinton was able to transform the typical image of mother as nurturer and caretaker to leader. While in the past, other scholars have noted that politicians use their families as a method of conveying policy positions, Clinton changed this. Using the discourse from the 2016 Democratic National Convention, Greenlee and VanSickle-Ward discuss how motherhood was used as a catalyst for a multidimensional appeal. Where it used to be the case that presenting a candidate as a mother was about courting the motherhood voting bloc, that was no longer the only goal. The status of being a mother, now, was used to inspire confidence and trust—particularly for taking on the position of Commander-in-Chief. Clinton worked to turn having children into a strength for the highest office in the land by making it a symbol of power and credibility. Motherhood was now about advocacy and expertise on issues, like women's issues, that once was of second tier importance.

In addition to imparting lessons for how women candidates might combat stereotypes that harm them and embrace those that help them, another major contribution from Clinton and her campaign was the recognition of and outreach to voters of color. Adrian Pantoja argues that Clinton's campaign marked a turning point for the study of Latina/o Politics. In his contribution, we learn that prior scholarship on the mobilization of the Latina/o community was primarily focused on the effects of fear, particularly fear stemming from restrictive immigration policies. However, according to Pantoja, Clinton's hiring of two key Latinas, in positions that were designed to work on mobilization efforts, shows that getting Latinas/os politically engaged is not just about fear. Clinton was able to tap into what many previous candidates had not—authentic targeting for the purpose of mobilizing the Latino/a community. The Latina/o vote was not merely about a Trump effect; it was due to a Hillary Effect based on effective political strategy.

In her piece titled "Latinas and Clinton's 2016 campaign," Christina Bejarano picks up where Pantoja leaves off, highlighting how Clinton worked to receive support from Latina voters. According to Bejarano, the increasing number of voters from the Latina/o community was message enough for Clinton to realize that if she was going to win, she would need this subgroup of women. Bejarano states that Clinton's hiring of Amanda Renteria as the national political director for Latina/o mobilization, and Lorella Praeli as the Latina/o Outreach director, enabled the campaign to present Clinton in an authentic way. Given that the Latina/o gender gap was a difference of 15 percent with 86 percent of Latinas voting for Clinton, it became clear that hiring a diverse campaign staff can yield positive results with targeted communities.

Finally, the contributions in Part 3 speak to the effects of Hillary Clinton on electoral politics in the aftermath of the presidential election. Lorrie Frasure digs deeper into the gender gap discussed by Bejarano. She begins by explaining that while many were deliberating about the importance of the women's vote during this election cycle, she knew that this messaging needed to be tempered, especially given that women as a group are quite diverse in their preferences and behavior. In terms of voting behavior, women of color supported Clinton in 2016, and their support for her was overwhelming. However, the majority of white women did not show up for Clinton; they supported her opponent. For Frasure, this was not a surprise because more white women than women of color identify as Republican. Consequently, the gender gap that is so often discussed where women vote more in favor of the Democratic Party than do men is actually mainly comprised of women of color. Overall, Frasure teaches us that women are not a monolithic group.

Finally, while there is much attention being paid to the Trump effect post-2016, there has been a lack of understanding and discussion behind the groundbreaking path that Clinton blazed for women vying for electoral office. In short, in running for the president, Clinton may have served as a role model, inspiring others to run. In her contribution, the President of Emerge A'shanti F. Gholar, explains how the Hillary effect is in part about "women refusing to sit idly by." In her piece Gholar details how the day after the 2016 presidential election Emerge was inundated by emails and phone messages from women wanting to run for political office. As she states, women began to ask themselves, if not Hillary then who? These women all realized it would have to be them who would have to step up, run for office and become change agents.

City Councilwoman Denise Davis provides an example of what Gholar depicts in her chapter. Davis begins by describing the inspiration she has felt from Clinton since she was a young child and the latter was the First Lady. She discusses the acute pain she and her friends felt after Clinton's loss because it was as if all the strides she thought women had made were now lost again. As Davis notes, this was why she spent the bulk of the next two years figuring out if she was going to run for local office or not.

The contribution by Kristin Kanthak examines how Clinton's run for office may have affected women's political ambition on a broader scale.

This contribution gives us a sense of how this moment in history may come to influence the emergence of women candidates in the future. In her study, Kanthak and her co-author, analyzed the general population and found that exposure to advertisements by Clinton increased women's political ambition, but only among those who had positive evaluations of her. The content of the advertisement was irrelevant. Simply seeing a prominent woman role model run for office increased ambition. And given the design of the study, these effects are distinctive to Clinton, and are not linked to Trump.

References

Anzia, S.F. and C.R. Berry (2011), "The Jackie (and Jill) Robinson Effect: Why Do Congresswomen Outperform Congressmen?" *American Journal of Political Science*, 55 (3): 478–93.

Bauer, N. (2018), "Running Local: Gender Stereotyping and Female Candidates in LocalElections," *Urban Affairs Review*, DOI: 10.1 1177/1078087418770807: 1–28.

Dittmar, K. (2015), *Navigating Gendered Terrain: Stereotypes and Strategy in Political Campaigns*, Philadelphia, PA: Temple University Press.

Dolan, K. (2014), "Gender Stereotypes, Candidate Evaluations, and Voting for Women Candidates: What Really Matters?," *Political Research Quarterly*, 67 (1): 96–107.

Eagly, A. H., M. Makhijani, and B. G. Klonsky (1992), "Gender and the Evaluation of Leaders: A Meta-Analysis," *Psychological Bulletin*, 111 (1): 233–56.

Fox, R. L. and J. L. Lawless (2011), "Gaining and Losing Interest in Running for Public Office: The Concept of Dynamic Political Ambition," *The Journal of Politics*, 73 (2): 443–62.

Hawkesworth, M. "Congressional Enactments of Race-Gender: Toward a Theory of Race-Gendered Institutions," *The American Political Science Review*, 97 (4): 529–50.

Herrnson, P.S., J. C. Lay, and A. K. Stokes (2003), "Women Running 'as Women': Candidate Gender, Campaign Issues, and Voter-Targeting Strategies," *The Journal of Politics*, 65 (1): 244–55.

Jalalzai, F. (2018), "A Comparative Assessment of Hillary Clinton's 2016 Presidential Race," *Socius: Sociological Research for a Dynamic World*, 4: 1–11.

Johnson, S. K., S. E. Murphy, S. Zewdie, and R. J. Reichard (2006), "The Strong, Sensitive Type: Effects of Gender Stereotypes and Leadership Prototypes on the Evaluation of Male and Female Leaders," *Organizational Behavior and Human Decision Processes*, 106: 39–60.

Larson, S. G. (2001), "Running as Women?," *Women & Politics*, 22 (2): 107–24.

Lazarus, J. and A. Steigerwalt (2018), *Gendered Vulnerability: How Women Work Harder to Stay in Office*, Ann Arbor: University of Michigan Press.

Meyer, M. C. (2013), 'Gendered Recruitment Without Trying: How Local Party Recruiters Affect Women's Representation', *Politics & Gender*, 9 (4): 390–413.

15

Hillary Clinton

The Exception and the Rule

Carrie Skulley

Political pundits and academics agree: Hillary Clinton has had a profound impact on American politics. Indeed, over the course of the past two decades, Hillary Clinton has changed our collective perception of what is possible for women in politics. Clinton's time as a public figure can be characterized in two ways. On the one hand, Clinton's experience represents a growing public acceptance for women's participation in national-level politics. On the other hand, academic studies document Clinton's experience as uniquely opposite of many other women's electoral and political experiences. In essence, Clinton embodies an interesting paradox: she is both the exception and the rule when it comes to women in politics. Her journey teaches us that while women are increasingly accepted into the political fold, trailblazers are frequently martyrs to the status quo.

Clinton was instrumental in contributing to the normalization of women as political entities. She has been a public figure for decades and in each of her roles, she has demonstrated that women's voices belong in politics and that women can excel in political roles. Popular accounts of Clinton's time as First Lady credit her with building on the Eleanor Roosevelt model for the office (e.g., Baker and Chozick 2014). That is, Clinton was more interested in being a policy wonk than filling the more traditional ceremonial and hospitality-oriented roles associated with the Office of First Lady. This trait was best exemplified when Clinton attempted healthcare reform in the 1990s. Although her plan for universal healthcare was ultimately unsuccessful, her plan demonstrated a policy-oriented drive that foreshadowed her career as both a Senator and Secretary of State.

Before leaving her position as First Lady, Hillary Clinton ran for and won a New York Senate seat (replacing Daniel Patrick Moynihan who was retiring).

Her victory represented the first time a First Lady sought and won elective office (Getlin 2000) *and* the first time New York sent a woman as part of its Senate delegation (Wasniewski 2007). During her eight years in the Senate, Clinton distinguished herself by being the first New York Senator to serve on the Senate Armed Services Committee and a champion of women's, children's and veteran's issues, especially as they related to healthcare (Wasniewski 2007). When Clinton joined the Obama administration as Secretary of State, she continued to focus on the rights of women and girls (Mead 2014) and placed an emphasis on addressing "poverty, the environment, education, and family planning" (Kristof 2014). When she left the post in 2013, she had logged more travel miles than any Secretary of State before her.

In 2016, Hillary Clinton ran for president for a second time (after losing in the Democratic Primary to Barack Obama in 2008). Adding her tenure as Secretary of State to an already impressive résumé, Clinton was arguably among the most qualified candidates ever to seek the office of the presidency (Nelson 2016). Despite winning the popular vote, she lost the Electoral College and Donald J. Trump became the 45th president of the United States. Although it is unlikely Hillary Clinton will be president of the United States, it is still fair to say that she has been instrumental in demonstrating that no political goal is beyond reach for women. Clinton has moved from First Lady to Senator, to Secretary of State, to presidential candidate. In this way, she is the rule. She demonstrates all that is possible.

Clinton's experience is seemingly consistent with academic work focusing on women and politics. Most of these studies find that women do not face a significant disadvantage when running for elective office (e.g., Dolan 2014). In fact, studies often show that women perform just as well as men in elections and frequently outperform them once in office (e.g., Anzia and Berry 2011). However, upon closer inspection, it is clear that Clinton's campaigns are plagued with stereotypes, sexism and preoccupation with scandal.

Clinton's media portrayals over the years have been filled with sexist language and imagery. In both the 2008 and 2016 presidential primaries, Clinton was referenced in more informal ways than were her male competitors (Uscinski and Goren 2010; Skulley 2017). For example, print journalism reporting on Clinton's 2016 primary campaign frequently stripped Clinton of her accrued professional honorifics (e.g., Secretary of State) and referenced her husband, former president Bill Clinton, in a significant portion of her coverage (Skulley 2017). Clinton's media coverage is also generally more negative than her competitors. In political cartoons, Clinton is satirized as an emasculator; "the wife the husband wants to get rid of" (Templin 1999). In an analysis of Clinton's 2000 senate campaign, Scharrer (2002) finds that a disproportionate amount of Clinton's coverage focused on her character and accused her of having irredeemable personality flaws like being "power hungry" and "narcissistic" (Scharrer 2002: 400). Alongside these incidents of character assassination, Clinton was also receiving less policy-oriented coverage than her male competitors (Meeks 2013; Skulley 2017).

Moreover, despite the fact that Clinton has adapted her style of speech (Jones 2016) and appearance (Clinton 2017) to be more masculine, there exists a preoccupation with her femininity and its effects on her ability to govern. When Clinton "teared up" at a New Hampshire campaign event during the 2008 presidential primary, detractors and pundits alike wondered if Clinton was "cracking under the pressure" suggesting that she did not have the emotional stamina to sustain a campaign (Curnalia and Mermer 2014). This concern about stamina was resurrected in 2016 when rumors swirled about Clinton's health after she suffered a coughing fit at a speaking engagement (Crockett 2016).

Uniquely negative portrayals of Hillary Clinton are not reserved for the traditional media and punditry; they exist among voters as well. In social media, Clinton is often depicted as "monstrous and/or cyborgian" (Ritchie 2012). In the most recent presidential election, Clinton's campaign was plagued with "fake news" stories that propagated conspiracy theories about child trafficking (Kang 2016) and murder (Eltagouri 2017). These "fake news" stories, combined with dissatisfaction over the outcome of the Benghazi hearings (Herszenhorn 2016) and preoccupation with Clinton's "missing emails" (Shane and Schmidt 2015), fomented anti-Clinton ire in a way no other candidate (or woman) has ever faced.

The fact that Hillary Clinton has achieved so much, despite the opposition she faces from all corners of the electorate, is remarkable. Hillary Clinton's journey can be thought of as inspirational but also as a cautionary tale. Clinton's experience teaches us that women's roles as political leaders are indeed expanding. Women can aspire to lead our country. But Clinton's experience also shows us that there exists extreme hostility toward women who are trailblazers. Whether or not we agree with her politics, we owe her a debt of thanks for bearing this burden so that future generations of women won't have to.

References

Anzia, Sa. F. and C. R. Berry (2011), "The Jackie (and Jill) Robinson Effect: Why Do Congresswomen Outperform Congressmen?" *American Journal of Political Science*, 55: 478–93.

Baker, P. and A. Chozick (2014), "Hillary Clinton's History as First Lady: Powerful, but Not Always Deft," *The New York Times*, https://www.nytimes.com/2014/12/06/us/politics/hillary-clintons-history-as-first-lady-powerful-but-not-always-deft.html (accessed August 1, 2018).

Clinton, H. R. (2017), *What Happened*, New York, NY: Simon & Schuster.

Crockett, E. (2016), "There's a Subtle Sexism in Asking Excessive 'Questions' About Hillary Clinton's Health," *Vox*, https://www.vox.com/2016/9/13/12891310/hillary-clinton-pneumonia-sexism-questions (accessed August 19, 2018).

Curnalia, R. M. L. and D. L. Mermer (2014), "The 'Ice Queen' Melted and It Won Her the Primary: Evidence of Gender Stereotypes and the Double Bind in News Frames of Hillary Clinton's 'Emotional Moment'," *Qualitative Research Reports in Communication*, 15: 26–32.

Dolan, K. (2014), "Gender Stereotypes, Candidate Evaluations, and Voting for Women Candidates: What Really Matters?," *Political Research Quarterly*, 67: 96–107.

Eltagouri, M. (2017), "Brother of Slain DNC Staffer Seth Rich Sues Right-Wing Activists, Newspaper over Conspiracy Theories," *The Washington Post*, https://www.washingtonpost.com/news/local/wp/2018/03/27/brother-of-slain-dnc-staffer-seth-rich-sues-right-wing-activists-newspaper-over-conspiracy-theories/?noredirect=on&utm_term=.b46efabc0d25 (accessed August 19, 2018).

Getlin, J. (2000), "Historic First for a First Lady as Clinton Wins N.Y. Senate Race," *Los Angeles Times*, http://www.latimes.com/politics/la-na-clinton-senate-2000-20160511-snap-story.html (accessed August 1, 2018).

Herszenhorn, D. M. (2016), "House Benghazi Report Finds No New Evidence of Wrongdoing by Hillary Clinton," *The New York Times*, https://www.nytimes.com/2016/06/29/us/politics/hillary-clinton-benghazi.html (accessed August 19, 2018).

Jones, J. J. (2016), "Talk 'Like a Man': The Linguistic Styles of Hillary Clinton, 1992–2013," *Perspectives on Politics*, 14: 625–42.

Kang, C. (2016), "Fake News Onslaught Targets Pizzeria as Nest of Child-Trafficking," *The New York Times*, https://www.nytimes.com/2016/11/21/technology/fact-check-this-pizzeria-is-not-a-child-trafficking-site.html (accessed August 1, 2018).

Kristof, N. (2014), "Madam Secretary Made a Difference," *The New York Times*, https://www.nytimes.com/2014/06/08/opinion/sunday/madam-secretary-made-a-difference.html?hp&rref=opinion (accessed August 19, 2018).

Mead, W. R. (2014), "Was Hillary Clinton a Good Secretary of State?," *The Washington Post*, https://www.washingtonpost.com/opinions/was-hillary-clinton-a-good-secretary-of-state/2014/05/30/16daf9c0-e5d4-11e3-a86b-362fd5443d19_story.html?utm_term=.dfef49abfc1a (accessed August 19, 2018).

Meeks, L. (2013), "All the Gender That"s Fit to Print: How the *New York Times* Covered Hillary Clinton and Sarah Palin in 2008," *Journalism & Mass Communication Quarterly*, 90: 520–39.

Nelson, L. (2016), "Is Hillary Clinton Really the Most Qualified Candidate? An Investigation," *Vox*, https://www.vox.com/2016/8/1/12316646/hillary-clinton-qualified (accessed August 1, 2018).

Ritchie, J. (2012), "Creating a Monster: Online Media Constructions of Hillary Clinton During the Democratic Primary Campaign, 2007–8," *Feminist Media Studies*, 13: 102–19.

Scharrer, E. (2002), "An 'Improbable Leap': A Content Analysis of Newspaper Coverage of Hillary Clinton's Transition from First Lady to Senate Candidate," *Journalism Studies*, 3: 393–406.

Shane, S. and M. S. Schmidt (2015), "Hillary Clinton Emails Take Long Path to Controversy," *The New York Times*, https://www.nytimes.com/2015/08/09/us/hillary -clinton-emails-take-long-path-to-controversy.html (accessed 1 August 2018).

Skulley, C. (2017), "'You Should Smile More!' Gender and Press Coverage of Candidates During the 2016 Presidential Primary," in J. Kraybill (ed.), *Unconventional, Partisan, and Polarizing Rhetoric: How the 2016 Election Shaped the Way Candidates Strategize, Engage, and Communicate*, 59–80, Lanham, MD: Lexington Books.

Templin, C. (1999), "Hillary Clinton as Threat to Gender Norms: Cartoon Images of the First Lady," *Journal of Communication Inquiry*, 23: 20–36.

Uscinski, J. E. and L. J. Goren (2010), "What's in a Name? Coverage of Senator Hillary Clinton During the 2008 Democratic Primary," *Political Research Quarterly*, 64: 884–96.

Wasniewski, M. (2007), *Women in Congress 1917–2006*, Washington, DC: Joint Committee on Printing.

16

Battling Stereotypes of Women as Weak on National Security

Mirya R. Holman, Jennifer L. Merolla, and Elizabeth J. Zechmeister

Devastating terrorist attacks abroad (Paris, November 13, 2015) and at home (San Bernardino, December 2, 2015) punctuated the last stretch of the invisible presidential primary period leading up to the 2016 presidential election, causing the issue to loom large with the Iowa caucus around the corner in January. Terrorism remained salient throughout the election year in 2016, as terrorists carried out major attacks in London, Brussels and Orlando, and various other threats and plots were discussed and (some) thwarted. Some speculated that elevated terrorist threat would advantage Clinton, given her national security experience (e.g., Albertson and Gadarian 2016) and the relative inexperience of some of her foremost challengers (Bernie Sanders and Donald Trump).

While we agree that Clinton should have held an advantage on the issue of terrorism, we argue that her extensive resume in national security primarily abated disadvantages on the issue that stem from her gender and partisanship. This may strike some as a negative reading of the election, especially compared to the other contributions in this volume. Our core contention, though, is that Clinton is a role model for how Democratic women can counter a public bias that favors Republican men on issues of national security.

Why are women, to begin with, at a disadvantage when vying for leadership roles in contexts in which security issues dominate the headlines? Scholars argue that voters have stereotypes of men and women, and they apply these to their evaluations of political candidates. According to social role theory, stereotypes emerge from the different roles that men and women occupy in society. As noted by Schneider and Bos (2019: 175), "These roles originated historically because of biological differences: Men's strength and women's childbearing meant that men occupied roles associated with hunting and laboring in the public sphere while women reared children and maintained home life." These general roles persisted with the shift to the industrial economy. Because of these different social roles, cultural norms developed that nurtured women's adoption of more communal traits, such as being compassionate, caring and having stronger interpersonal skills, which would be useful to their caregiving role, while men were rewarded for more agentic traits, such as being strong, assertive and aggressive, which would be useful to their economic roles, and in turn as leaders. Scholars have found that voters extend some of these stereotypes to perceptions of the traits that women and men carry into political leadership, and also draw on these trait stereotypes to make inferences about the types of issues each is better able to handle: men in office are seen as better able to handle foreign affairs, crime and defense, while women are perceived as better able to handle children, family, education and women's issues (Sanbonmatsu 2002; Bauer 2015, 2018; Holman, Merolla, and Zechmeister 2011, 2016). While some of these stereotypes may help women candidates, they may serve as a liability when issues like terrorism are relevant. In general, women are perceived as less able to handle the issue and voters tend to prefer stronger (more agentic) leaders in such a context (Merolla and Zechmeister 2009).

The public's associations of the comparative strengths and weaknesses of political parties can boost or counteract gender biases in leadership evaluations. While the Democratic Party has a strong reputation on handling issues like healthcare, "women's" issues and welfare, Republicans "own" national security and free market economic issues (Petrocik 1996; Ondercin 2017). It is common for Democratic women to receive especially high marks on issues that align with stereotypes of their gender and party (such as healthcare), while they are downgraded on foreign policy and national defense (Holman, Merolla, and Zechmeister 2016; Bauer 2018). At the same time, women running under the Republican label can find that their partisanship immunizes them against disadvantages on national security that owe to their gender (Holman, Merolla, and Zechmeister 2016; Bauer 2018). These dynamics linking gender biases and party reputations may be especially pronounced in contests for executive offices, where party is particularly salient and there is a higher baseline preference for candidates with masculine characteristics (Kenski and Falk 2004; Conroy 2015; Sanbonmatsu 2002).

Given the shadow that terrorist threat cast over 2016, we might expect that Hillary Clinton—as a woman, a Democrat, and as a candidate for the US presidency—faced an insurmountable obstacle in breaking the highest, hardest political glass ceiling. Our own research shows that women on the left, including

Clinton in years prior to her tenure as Secretary of State, are evaluated less positively, especially with respect to perceptions of leadership, to the degree that terrorism is salient. In one experiment-based study conducted against the backdrop of the 2004 election, we found that a group randomly assigned to read a news story about the threat of terrorism reported lower evaluations of then-Senator Clinton, compared to those who did not read the article (Holman, Merolla, and Zechmeister 2011). Meanwhile, we found that Secretary of State Condoleezza Rice—a Republican woman—received higher evaluations. In short, Clinton faced a double bind due to her gender and partisanship, while Rice was able to overcome the disadvantage of gender by being from a party perceived as strong on terrorism (and possibly also as a result of her experience in national security leadership). We observed similar patterns for gender and partisanship in a later experiment-based study that asked participants to evaluate hypothetical politicians (Holman, Merolla, and Zechmeister 2016).

Is there any way out of the double bind that confronts Democratic women? Here, Clinton's example is instructive, for it highlights the value of cultivating expertise in national security.[1] Early in her Senate career, Clinton established a reputation as a policy wonk in the domain of national security, in part by joining the armed services committee. As columnist Mark Landler recounts, "After 9/11, Clinton saw Armed Services as better preparation for her future. For a politician looking to hone hard-power credentials—a woman who aspired to be commander in chief—it was the perfect training ground. She dug in like a grunt at boot camp."[2] While it would take time for the public to become aware of her increased expertise on national security, she gained the respect of foreign policy elites.[3] That base became a launching pad off which Clinton transitioned to Secretary of State under the Obama administration. In that more visible role, Clinton made further inroads in cultivating a reputation for experience and leadership in national security issues.

This strategy paid dividends according to data from studies we conducted after Clinton served as Secretary of State. With an experiment-based design similar to our earlier scholarship on the topic, we found much weaker negative effects, and in some studies, no negative effect, of reading about terrorism on evaluations of Clinton's leadership qualities (Holman, Merolla, and Zechmeister 2017). We also found a small net positive effect for Clinton's leadership evaluations among participants who were asked to read a more comprehensive news story about terrorist threat that included discussion of Clinton's experience on the issue and Donald Trump's lack of experience. Interestingly, the boost to Clinton from that news story was particularly pronounced among Republican men.

In sum, what Hillary Clinton has demonstrated is that Democratic women—by acquiring experience and cultivating reputations in national security—can tamp down on the tendency for the public to perceive women on the left as weaker options when terrorist or related threats are elevated. Our research suggests that such a strategy can even boost positive impressions among the most unlikely of allies (Republican men). As she has done in many other ways, Clinton's smart and deliberate efforts to overcome obstacles has helped blaze new paths for women candidates to come. In fact, the lessons Clinton has imparted are already being put into practice. In the 2018 midterms—particularly in districts that have typically leaned Republican—a record number of Democratic women veterans ran for office, and a number of them were successful in those bids.

References

Albertson, B. and S. K. Gadarian (2016), "Anxiety over Terrorism Advantages Hillary Clinton," *Political Communication*, 33 (4): 681–5.

Bauer, N. M. (2015), "Emotional, Sensitive, and Unfit for Office? Gender Stereotype Activation and Support Female Candidates," *Political Psychology*, 36 (6): 691–708.

Bauer, N. M. (2018), "Untangling the Relationship Between Partisanship, Gender Stereotypes, and Support for Female Candidates," *Journal of Women, Politics & Policy*, 39 (1): 1–25.

Conroy, M. (2015), *Masculinity, Media, and the American Presidency*, New York: Palgrave Macmillan.

Holman, M. R., J. L. Merolla, and E. J. Zechmeister (2011), "Sex, Stereotypes, and Security: A Study of the Effects of Terrorist Threat on Assessments of Female Leadership," *Women, Politics, and Policy*, 32 (3): 173–92.

Holman, M. R., J. L. Merolla, and E. J. Zechmeister (2016), "Terrorist Threat, Male Stereotypes, and Candidate Evaluations," *Political Research Quarterly*, 69 (1): 134–47.

Holman, M. R., J. L. Merolla, and E. J. Zechmeister (2017), "Can Experience Overcome Stereotypes in Times of Terror Threat?," *Research & Politics*, 4 (1): 1–7, doi:10.1177/2053168016688121.

Kenski, K. and E. Falk (2004), "Of What Is That Glass Ceiling Made? — A Study of Attitudes About Women and the Oval Office," *Women & Politics*, 26 (2): 57–80.

Merolla, J. L. and E. J. Zechmeister (2009), *Democracy at Risk: How Terrorist Threats Affect the Public*, Chicago: University of Chicago Press.

Ondercin, H. L. (2017), "Who Is Responsible for the Gender Gap? The Dynamics of Men's and Women's Democratic Macropartisanship, 1950–2012," *Political Research Quarterly*, 70 (4): 749–77.

Petrocik, J. R. (1996), "Issue Ownership in Presidential Elections: With a 1980 Case Study," *American Journal of Political Science*, 40 (3): 825–50.

Sanbonmatsu, K. (2002), "Gender Stereotypes and Vote Choice," *American Journal of Political Science*, 46: 20–34.

Schneider, M. C. and A. L. Bos (2019), "The Application of Social Role Theory to the Study of Gender and Politics," *Advances in Political Psychology*, 40 (1): 173–213.

17

Rethinking Gender as an Electoral Asset

Kelly Dittmar

In 2008, I was frustrated. Working toward my PhD in women and American politics while employed at the Center for American Women and Politics (CAWP) at Rutgers University, I was tasked with analyzing the gender dynamics of the 2008 election in real time. I saw the Clinton campaign's gender confusion from the start. A later-leaked memo from Clinton's campaign strategist confirmed what I expected all along: prominent members of her team perceived Clinton's gender as a hurdle to overcome en route to the presidency instead of an asset to her candidacy. The country is open to the "first father being a woman," Clinton campaign strategist Mark Penn wrote in that memo, but not ready for a 'first mama' president. Based on that assessment, Clinton's 2008 campaign focused more on proving she was man enough to be president instead of discussing the ways in which being a woman might be a value-added in the Oval Office.

My frustration with what I perceived as a missed opportunity to challenge the masculine dominance of the presidency inspired a dissertation-then-book on how political practitioners addressed gender in strategic decision-making. At the end of that book, I suggested that candidates and campaign practitioners need to take seriously their ability to disrupt political institutions by offering voters new images of and credentials for officeholding. Instead of simply giving voters what they want (or what they expect), campaign elites can push voters to rethink their expectations of both gender and candidacy.

For decades, women candidates have sought to navigate the incongruity between voters' expectations of gender—which assume women hold stereotypically feminine traits and areas of expertise—and candidacy—which favor traits and expertise most often associated with masculinity and men. Women candidates have often adapted to a man's world of American politics by working to prove their masculine credentials—on both traits and issue expertise—in making their case to voters. They have found success in this strategy, winning elections and (slowly) increasing their presence across levels of elective office. But disrupting political institutions requires more than women's presence; when women challenge the credentials and qualifications deemed most valuable to officeholding, they create opportunities for candidates whose identities, experiences, and expertise have been undervalued and underrepresented in US political history—which is a history in which upper-class, white, heterosexual men have held the greatest concentration of power.

It is this disruption that will yield the long-term change necessary to alter the imbalance of power in American politics that has long advantaged white, heterosexual men. At the start of her 1981 book *In the Running*, Ruth Mandel—CAWP's founding director, wrote, "Almost nowhere does the shift in traditional values and patterns of female behavior stand out in sharper relief than in the picture of a woman stepping forward in the political arena to announce forthrightly, 'I'm the candidate.'" By 2015, I wanted to see a different shift, one in which the traditional values and patterns of candidate behavior would be both illuminated and questioned when a candidate stepped forward to announce, "I'm a woman."

Hillary Clinton did that. In 2015, she told an audience of campaign supporters: "I'm not asking you to vote for me because I'm a woman. I'm asking you to vote for me on the merits." But, unlike in her 2008 presidential bid—where she repeatedly affirmed that she was not "running as a woman"—she added in 2015, "But one of those merits is that I'm a woman." On the campaign trail, Clinton talked about her intimate understanding of the challenges facing working mothers and described the sexism she confronted on her path to professional success, while simultaneously recognizing how her race and class privilege distinguished her experiences from other women. In those campaign moments, Clinton—whether intentionally or not—challenged us all to question why the distinctive perspectives that come from experiencing life as a woman in the United States are not equally valuable to agenda-setting and deliberation as are other unique professional experiences (e.g., military, business) that we have long valued in candidates and officeholders.

To be sure, Hillary Clinton was not the first woman candidate to discuss the value of being a woman. Women candidates had for decades been offering new models of candidacy and officeholding before her name was on the presidential ballot, drawing from distinct life experiences as caregivers, trailblazers, and political outsiders to appeal to voters. But Clinton was upending the gendered rules of the game at the highest level and in competition for the most masculine office in American politics, and she was embracing being a woman against an opponent who was unapologetic in his belief that the best—and manliest—man should win. It was in that contrast that Clinton ensured that the deep-seated gender biases of presidential politics would be exposed. And it was in the shift from 2008 to 2016 in how Clinton campaigned for the presidency that she illuminated the potential for progress in seeing both the cultural and electoral value of embracing gender as a woman candidate.

In 2018, women candidates benefited from and built upon this disruption of campaign norms in the ways in which they made their case for candidacy and officeholding. Their unapologetic embrace of their experiences as women and the diversity with which they navigated and performed gender will have lasting effects, regardless of their victory or defeat on Election Day.

Hillary Clinton's candidacies were neither the start nor the end to this transformation of the gendered terrain of campaigns, but in writing the history of women disrupting the status quo in electoral politics, Clinton's legacy will shine bright.

Reference

Mandel, R. B. (1981), *In the Running: The New Woman Candidate*, New Haven, CT: Ticknor and Fields.

A Mother for President

Motherhood Takes Center Stage at the DNC

Rachel VanSickle-Ward and Jill S. Greenlee

A century ago motherhood was frequently invoked to argue against giving women the right to vote in the United States. If women entered the political arena, it was claimed, they would abandon their natural duty to their children, with disastrous consequences for everyone involved. In 2016, Hillary Clinton ran unabashedly as a mother, and in so doing, helped change the conversation around motherhood, expertise, leadership and politics. Perhaps the clearest example of this was the 2016 Democratic National Convention (DNC), where motherhood was presented as a central plank in the effort to convince Americans to elect our first woman president. As Greenlee (2014) found in her book, motherhood has been used in a variety of ways to connect women to politics and justify women's voices. And yet we have never seen motherhood quite so forcefully linked to presidential power, in support of a candidate who is herself a mother.

References to motherhood at the Democratic convention were ubiquitous. The First Lady, Michele Obama, linked motherhood to trust and advocacy: "I trust Hillary to lead this country because I've seen her lifelong devotion to our nation's children—not just her own daughter, who she has raised to perfection, but every child who needs a champion."[1] President Obama invoked Clinton's maternal roles as he described her as a multidimensional leader: "This fighter, this stateswoman, this mother and grandmother, this public servant this patriot."[2] Hillary Clinton's own daughter offered more personal references to Clinton's motherhood, relating intimate details of a mother who was nurturing, committed and available despite a non-traditional career path.[3]

And there were other mothers at the Democratic convention as well. The nine African American "The Mothers of the Movement" women who lost their children to gun violence and police aggression tied their own political activism as mothers to Clinton's political leadership.[4] Geneva Reed-Veal, Sandra Bland's mother, stated "I am here with Hillary Clinton tonight because she is a leader and a mother who will say our children's names." Lucy McBath, mother of Jordan Davis, argued that Clinton "isn't afraid to sit at a table with grieving mothers and bear the full force of our anguish." Sybrina Fulton, who spoke of her son, Trayvon Martin, explained that Clinton "has the compassion and understanding to support grieving mothers, she has the courage to lead the fight for common sense gun legislation." These testimonies conveyed two powerful and interrelated messages: motherhood motivates the advocacy and political action of these women and these women view Clinton's strength and solidarity as a function of her own role as a mother.

Appeals to motherhood in politics is not new. Elder and Green (2011) find that the family has become a common vehicle for the two major political parties to convey their policy preferences. And Greenlee (2014) finds, framing their appeals around motherhood in particular has been a common way for the parties to reach out to women voters since they won the franchise in 1920. Senator Patty Murray (D-WA) famously campaigned as "a mom in tennis shoes" (Wilson 2011). Former governor and Republican vice-presidential candidate Sarah Palin (2008) called herself a "hockey mom" and, as a mother of a child with Down syndrome, spoke publicly on issues facing children who have special needs.

But then there was the 2016 DNC. Never before have we witnessed the presidential nominee of a major party who was a mother—and who said so loudly and proudly. In the past, discourse around motherhood in presidential politics was meant to appeal to mothers as a voting bloc or to offer some personal insights to the lives of male candidates who were sons, fathers, and husbands. But motherhood itself had never before been used as a credential for the position of commander-in-chief.

The candidate herself directly linked her identity to policy positions and expertise on "women's issues" that have traditionally been secondary in presidential campaigns.[5] In accepting the nomination, she included a line that has long been a staple of her stump speech: "If fighting for affordable child care and paid family leave is playing the 'woman card,' then Deal Me In!" This phrase is more than a catchy slogan, it is a powerful rebuke to the idea that emphasizing gender is a distraction from "normal" politics. And it is striking message in a culture that too often assumes that mothers are less competent in the workplace.[6]

Promoting motherhood as a source of power, strength and credibility in politics, or in any other arena, is not without peril. It can essentialize women who are mothers, promoting a one-dimensional view of their identity as a nurturing caretaker above all else. It can be used as a cudgel for women who are not mothers, reinforcing a dangerous and reductive message that becoming a mother is the key to "true womanhood." Some attempts to empower mothers rely on a cookie-cutter heteronormative version of family or serve to diminish other caretakers. Moreover, while motherhood can bring a sense of connection and solidarity from shared experience, we recognize that it is far from a universal experience. While it may be touching to hear that Chelsea Clinton is proud of her mom, we know that the experience of mothering has been quite different for women with less privilege.

Potential pitfalls notwithstanding, motherhood continues to shape politics in profound ways. In 2018, Lucy McBath grounded her successful campaign for a congressional seat in Georgia in her experience as mother, and continues to center that identity in her legislative work on preventing gun violence.[7] Speaker of the house Nancy Pelosi, the first woman to serve in that role, frequently credits her experience as a mother and grandmother for honing her strategic acumen.[8] Perhaps the clearest evidence of the ground broken by Clinton is found in Senator Kirsten Gillibrand, who fully embraced motherhood in her presidential campaign, promising to "fight for your children as hard as I would fight for my own,"[9] and stating, "I'm not a candidate who happens to be a mom; being a mom is a big part of what I'm running for."[10]

Complicated and perilous as it may be, it is powerful to see mothers take center stage in national politics. Mothers' work has long been devalued, and mothers' policy claims have long been ignored. To many mothers, and to those who have supported and appreciated them, it was surely empowering to hear Clinton, the first woman nominated for president by a major party, accept that nomination with the words: "Standing here as my mother's daughter, and my daughter's mother, I'm so happy this day has come."

References

Elder, L. and S. Greene (2011), "The Politics of Parenthood: Parenthood Effects on Issue Attitudes and Candidate Evaluations in 2008," *American Politics Research*, 40 (3): 419–49.

Greenlee, J. S. (2014), *The Political Consequences of Motherhood*, Ann Arbor, MI: University of Michigan Press.

Palin, S. (2008), "Palin's Speech on Children with Special Needs," *Real Clear Politics*, https://www.realclearpolitics.com/articles/2008/10/palins_speech_on_children_with.html.

Wilson, R. (2011), "From 'Mom in Tennis Shoes' to One of the Nation's Most Powerful Democrats," *The Atlantic*, https://www.theatlantic.com/politics/archive/2011/08/from-mom-in-tennis-shoes-to-one-of-the-nations-most-powerful-democrats/243458/.

Turing Point

Hillary Clinton's Impact on Latino Politics

Adrian D. Pantoja

This chapter situates the 2016 election in the broader context of Latino political development. My own interest in Latino politics[1] began in 1994, when Proposition 187 appeared on the California ballot. In what is now a familiar script, Prop. 187 and Pete Wilson's gubernatorial campaign essentially blamed most of California's economic and social woes on undocumented immigrants. As a Mexican American residing in California at the time, this was my first experience with a racialized campaign directed at immigrants and Latinos more broadly, and it led me to become engaged with Latino politics on a personal and an academic level. The following analysis is informed by both this experience and the expertise I have acquired over the last two decades.

I argue that Hillary Clinton's campaign marked a turning point in Latino politics. The campaign incorporated and engaged Hispanic voters at a level not seen before, and Latino voters responded positively to these efforts by turning out in record numbers and voting for Clinton. Unfortunately, the success of Clinton's strategy with Latino voters has been overshadowed by bad polling data and a narrative that highlights Trump as a motivating factor for their political behavior in 2016. This chapter seeks to set the record straight.

The beginnings of Latino electoral politics can be traced back to the 1960 presidential election, when a group of Mexican American leaders from Texas formed Viva Kennedy Clubs. Their goal was a simple one: gain recognition by

---

[1] Throughout this chapter the terms "Latino" and "Hispanic" will be used interchangeably. Both are pan-ethnic labels that are used to group different Latin American ancestries under a single name. In certain states, like California, Latino is the preferred term, while Hispanic is widely used in Texas and New Mexico. Thus, the preference for either label will vary across states and among different segments of Latinos. Increasingly, millennial Latinos are embracing and popularizing the label Latinx in an effort to include transgender persons.

demonstrating the power of Mexican American voters. These leaders naively believed that Kennedy's victory would lead the political parties to take Latino voters seriously and thus direct greater campaign efforts toward engaging this electorate. Regrettably, Latino voters remained on the periphery of electoral politics for decades, despite the fact that Hispanic leaders continued to emphasize their growing political clout. Academics like Rodolfo de la Garza have long argued that the "power of the Latino vote" is both a myth and a hype. Over time, Latinos earned the label of "sleeping giant" because of their political weakness despite being the nation's largest minority group.

In 1994, Latinos in California began to shed that label following the passage of Prop. 187. Prop. 187 was the first in a series of anti-immigrant initiatives and campaigns that swept the nation. The initiative was designed to deny a wide range of public services to undocumented immigrants. Additionally, public servants were required to report suspected undocumented immigrants to the Immigration and Naturalization Service (INS). Republican governor Pete Wilson made Prop. 187 the hallmark of his campaign. Both campaigns were highly racialized. These highly racialized campaigns and initiatives eventually spurred Latinos to higher levels of political engagement. Research by Pantoja, Ramírez and Segura (2001) was the first to provide empirical evidence that Latinos in California were voting in record numbers. Turnout was particularly high among foreign-born Latinos.[1] The proverbial "sleeping giant" had awakened and, over time, Latino voters helped turn California into a solidly blue state.

Scholars and pundits examining the dramatic political changes in California believed that a threatening political context was a sufficient condition for activating Latino voters. This essentially narrowed political empowerment to a psychological process. In other words, turnout was largely attributed to a person's subjective emotional feelings or what psychologist call *affect*. Emotions, like fear and anger, have been found to induce a wide variety of political behaviors, including turning out to vote. A decade later, when the anti-immigration initiative Proposition 200 appeared in Arizona, it was widely assumed that Latinos would respond politically as they did in California. I essentially made similar arguments, at the time, as a professor at Arizona State University. When Latinos in Arizona failed to meet expectations, some scholars began to re-examine events in California. A second look at the political changes in California revealed that community-based organizations, nonprofits and labor unions played key roles in registering and mobilizing Latinos in the state. In short, direct mobilization efforts were pivotal in empowering the Latino electorate. This latter finding has largely been ignored by most scholars and pundits.

Despite Latinos' influence and power in California, pundits continued to regard them as insignificant when it came to influencing national politics. Hillary Clinton attempted to change this perception. After announcing her bid for the presidency in the spring of 2015, she made three important decisions that signaled her intention to take Latino voters seriously. First, she appointed Amanda Renteria, a California Latina, as the National Political Director of her campaign. Second, she hired the polling firm Latino Decisions to poll Latinos and improve her Latino outreach efforts. Her campaign strategy of mobilizing Latino voters and policy positions on immigration and other issues became a major draw for Hispanics. Third, she hired a record number of Latinos on her campaign staff, including Lorella Praeli, a DREAMer, as director of Latino outreach. The executive director of one of the largest pro-immigration organizations America's Voice noted that Praeli's hire was another bold move by Clinton to engage seriously with Latino voters.

During the fall of 2016, I ran an eight-week tracking poll leading up to Election Day for Latino Decisions. The results from that poll (Figure 19.1) clearly show Hillary Clinton surging ahead of Trump among Latino voters. By week 8, Clinton had a commanding 62-point lead among Latinos. In the end, Hillary won about 77 percent of the Latino vote, while Trump won a mere 18 percent according to Latino Decisions estimates. These estimates ran contrary to those found by the exit polls and other polling firms. According to this data, Latino turnout and support for Clinton was lower than that received by Obama in 2012. It was also claimed that Trump won 30 percent of the Latino vote, outperforming Mitt Romney in 2012. In an effort to debunk this bad data and results, scholars associated with Latino Decisions ran a series of statistical

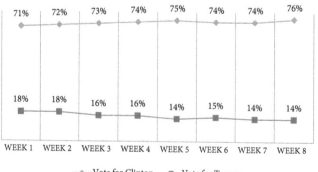

Figure 19.1 Latino vote choice in 2016.
(*Source*: Latino Decisions 2016 tracking poll, www.latinodecisions.com)

analysis in heavily Latino precincts. The results found that Latino turnout rates in these geographic areas were higher in 2016 than in 2012. Additional analysis by professor Francisco Pedraza of 864 heavily Latino precincts in Texas found that Hillary Clinton won more votes than Obama in 723 of them.[2] Yet, in the end, our analysis was drowned out in the cacophonous debate about what really happened in 2016.

A more compelling case for Clinton's Latino outreach strategy can be found if we look at the data analyzing mobilization efforts by the Democratic and Republican parties over time. In week 1 of the tracking poll, 39 percent of Latinos said they had been contacted to vote by a political party or candidate. By week 8 that figure jumped to 46 percent. When asked who had contacted them, 62 percent said it was someone from the Democratic Party, while mere 19 percent said it was someone from the Republican Party. Clearly, the Democratic Party, with Hillary's campaign leading these efforts, significantly outpaced Republicans when it came to mobilizing Latino voters.

There is no doubt in my mind that Latino voting behavior in 2016 was unprecedented. Latinos turned out and voted at high rates and overwhelmingly supported Clinton. Unfortunately, most post-election analysis of Latinos attributes this outcome to a so-called Trump effect—a reactive mobilization, induced by fear and anger, against Trump. In looking at Latino political behavior in California and Arizona, we now know that psychological factors, such as fear and anger, alone cannot explain the voting patterns of Latinos. A more compelling argument is that Latino turnout in 2016 was fueled by the Hillary Effect, an enthusiasm for Hillary Clinton and her Latino mobilization strategy. Clinton was unique among previous Democratic presidential candidates in that she actively sought to wake the "sleeping giant." In essence, Hillary Clinton helped realize the goals of the Viva Kennedy generation, fifty-six years later, by giving Latinos national recognition.

Reference

Pantoja, A. D., R. Ramírez and G. Segura. (2001), "Citizens by Choice, Voters by Necessity: Patterns in Political Mobilization by Naturalized Latinos," *Political Research Quarterly*, 54 (4): 729–50.

Latinas and Clinton's 2016 Campaign

Christina Bejarano

Clinton's experience in the 2016 presidential election pointed to growing debates over the importance and influence of identity politics. While Hillary Clinton benefited from several overarching and significant coalitions, she was still unable to effectively overcome significant gendered campaign obstacles. This discussion speaks to several important political developments during Clinton's campaign outreach toward Latinos. In particular, Clinton's novel "Latina-focused" campaign strategies have guided my own particular research on Latina politics. The Latina-specific campaign strategy to court Latino voters used Latina community leaders to reach out to their community for voter mobilization efforts. This was the first time a presidential candidate focused mobilization efforts specifically on Latinas.

The 2016 election marked the most diverse electorate in US history, with 31 percent of eligible voters from racial and ethnic minorities or a net increase of 7.5 million eligible voters.[1] In contrast, the share of the white, non-Hispanic eligible voters hit an all-time low of 69 percent. In particular, Latinos increased their number of eligible voters by another 4 million to reach a record setting 27.3 million eligible voters, which is the largest increase of any racial/ethnic group.[2] Despite these gains in the share of the electorate, many diverse potential voters also faced increased voter intimidation and suppression efforts.[3]

In spite of the voting obstacles in place, Latino voter turnout increased significantly compared to the 2012 election. It is estimated that 13 to 14 million Latinos voted in the election, which is an increase of 2 to 3 million since 2012.[4] Moreover, Latino voters overwhelmingly supported Hillary Clinton by an estimated 79 percent.[5] In fact, this Latino support of Clinton increased significantly compared to recent presidential elections when Democratic candidate Barack Obama won a substantial show of Latino support by more than 67 percent in 2008 and 72 percent in 2012.[6]

In the 2016 election, 54 percent of women and 41 percent of men supported the Democratic candidate Hillary Clinton, a 13-point gender gap.[7] Women were 12 points less likely than men to support Donald Trump, yielding a 12-point gender gap; this gender gap was up by two points from the 2012 election.[8] Among whites, the gender gap in support of Clinton was at 12 points (43 to 31 percent).[9] This follows the recent trend of the majority of white women, 53 percent, supporting the Republican presidential candidate instead of the Democratic candidate, which also happened in both 2008 and 2012.[10] While precedent would have predicted this behavior by white women, the results are contrary to some expectations that Clinton would receive more support from white women than previous Democratic nominees because they share both racial and gender identity.

This recent trend also highlights the growing role of women of color to reinforce the modern gender gap in the United States. Minority voters overwhelmingly supported Clinton, especially minority women. The 2016 gender gap in support of Clinton was 14 points among blacks (94 to 80 percent), which was 5 points larger than the gender gap in black voter support for Obama in 2012. Among Latinos, the gender gap in support for Clinton was 15 points (86 to 71 percent), a growth by 4 points compared to 2012.[11] Further, the gender gap in support of Clinton was 7 points among Asian Americans, with Democratic support coming from 79 percent of Asian American women compared to 72 percent of Asian American men.[12] In addition to the strong show of support for Clinton in the election by women of color, they also represent a growing electorate that will continue to have a more dramatic impact on American politics. So, when we talk about the modern gender gap in support of Democratic candidates, we need to focus on the growing role of minority women. In addition, throughout the campaign, a majority of Latinos, 75 percent, agreed that Hillary Clinton was the best candidate to unite Americans of all backgrounds. There was a gender gap with 80 percent of Latinas expressing support for Clinton as a unifier, compared to 70 percent of Latino males.[13]

Clinton's 2016 campaign featured a prominent role for Latinos, in particular for Latinas. The campaign employed Amanda Renteria as the national political director and Lorella Praeli as the Latino Outreach Director.[14] In addition, the DNC utilized several prominent Latinos/as for featured speakers during the national convention. Many prominent Latinas also served as campaign surrogates during the campaign, including former Miss Universe Alicia Machado. Trump's attacks on Machado included crude and racist remarks about women and Latinas in particular. This attack demonstrated Trump's lack of concern or even particular interest in campaign outreach toward Latinas.[15] Instead, Trump continued to further alienate the Latino community, Latinas specifically.

The Clinton campaign made several headways to diversifying the political campaign. In contrast to the Trump campaign's total absence of Spanish-language ads, the Clinton campaign began to run Spanish-language ads in Nevada and Florida late in the campaign, and they provided Spanish-language translation of her website.[16] There are also lessons learned from the campaign, including the need to incorporate more Latinos in the process as campaign staff, consultants, organizations, and as potential voters. In addition, the Clinton campaign highlighted potential pitfalls when attempting to court Latino voters, which point to the need to be more culturally aware and sensitive to diverse communities. For example, Clinton had some missteps in her campaign, especially as they relate to minority and women voters. The Clinton campaign received Latino backlash when they ran a list on the campaign website entitled "7 things Hillary Clinton has in common with your abuela," which implied Clinton can be compared to Latino grandmothers.[17] The social media backlash was made vocal through a series of twitter hashtags #NotMyAbuela #NotMiAbuela.

Overall, we continue to witness the long-lasting effect of Clinton's presidential campaign, including her efforts toward mobilizing more diverse communities. As these important constituencies continue to push to make their voices heard in politics, future political candidates would be wise to pay attention to their intersecting interests.

21

Not in "Mixed Company"?

Courageous Conversations About Women and the Race Gap in American Politics

Lorrie Frasure

A few months before the 2016 presidential election, I shared brunch in Malibu, California, with one of my best girlfriends visiting from Chicago, and three other women whom she invited to join us. We discussed the upcoming election and they queried me on whether Senator Clinton could win against Donald Trump. In the comfort of our "black girlfriends" oceanside table, I did not detail decades-old academic theories such as the role of partisanship, economic indicators, gender biases or the role of "intersecting identities" in American politics. Perhaps these factors were wrapped in my quick and worried response exclaiming, "if white women actually vote for her!" A collective mmm-hmm and head-nodding in agreement filled the table, followed by nervous laughter.

Senator Clinton's Electoral College loss forced an often-uncomfortable conversation about gender, race, and party politics in the United States. A difficult dialogue ensued in academic, policy and social media spaces following the 2016 election, confronting the role of gender, race, class, power, patriarchy, sexism and racism (Azari 2017; Bracic, Israel-Trummel and Shortle 2018; Frasure-Yokley 2018; Junn 2016; Roberts and Ely 2016; Rogers 2016; Ruiz-Grossman 2016). These conversations are often difficult to hold in so-called mixed company between women of color and white women, even progressive white women. By "not in mixed company," I refer to the urban dictionary's definition of this popular phrase: "A group of people in which a discussion of a certain topic would be taboo due to the presence of a person or people who might be offended by such a discussion."

While the gender and politics scholarship and the popular media often depicts women voters as a Democratic Party monolith, many scholars have long pointed out the hegemony of white womanhood to this narrative, often to the exclusion of the voices of women of color (Cathy 2003; Smooth 2006). However, the 2016 election brought to the fore the need for academic research and our everyday discourse to listen to and understand women across various backgrounds and identities.

More than two years following the 2016 election, academics, journalists, activists, and beauty salon patrons still ponder why so many white women chose Donald Trump over Hillary Clinton. The election of the 2016 Republican nominee pushed us to look beyond the monolith of "women voters" and to grapple with the ways in which white women historically behave politically different from women of color. It required us to examine how the persistence of a partisan gender gap between male and female voters in presidential campaigns is driven by the historical patterns of women of color voters, particularly black women in majority support of the Democratic Party candidates since the 1960s (Smooth 2006). White women, with few exceptions including 1964 and 1996, have been consistent supporters of Republican Party presidential candidates since the American National Election Study (ANES) began collecting data about US voters and their preferences in 1948 (Junn 2016; Smooth 2006; Tien 2017).

My retort during brunch was not that white women would be *the* deciding factor in clinching the Electoral College for Clinton, but rather reflected an understanding of white women's long-standing position in American politics. In 2016 White women voters were the single largest group of voters in the United States and held substantial electoral sway. It's logical, at least to Republican and Democratic Party strategists, that white women are the most sought-after swing voters in the electorate ("suburban voters," "soccer moms," "security moms").

Until the 2016 election, most existing academic studies of gender differences on vote choice were undifferentiated by race and ethnicity. The widespread bewilderment regarding the political behaviors and attitudes of white women is puzzling since much of the women and politics literature is based on data with large samples of white women across class, geography and other demographics (Cassese, Barnes and Branton 2015; Frasure-Yokley 2018). With the exception of a few sources such as the 2016 Collaborative Multiracial Post-Election Survey (CMPS), data collection efforts with specific attention to politics, and surveying large numbers of women of color, remains dismal. White women often remain the designated "reference category" for which the behaviors and attitudes of all women of color are often compared. In doing so, researchers fail to fully examine and understand white women's political behavior and attitudes. Scholarship in gender and politics that does not account for group differences in race/ethnicity may present misleading results, which are either underestimated, overestimated, or simply wrong.

Since 2016, my research examines how sexism, and race work in conjunction with gender to produce electoral outcomes. My article, "Choosing the Velvet Glove: Women Voters, Ambivalent Sexism, and Vote Choice in 2016" examined how ambivalent sexism toward women influenced vote choice among American women during the 2016 presidential election. Ambivalent sexism moves beyond old-fashioned sexism or gender discrimination. The theory is the result of two persistent facts about relations between men and women: male dominance (patriarchy) and interdependence between the sexes (Glick and Fiske 1997, 2001, 1996). It is an ideology composed of measures of "hostile sexism" and "benevolent sexism." Hostile sexism reflects negative or antagonistic evaluations and stereotypes about women (e.g., most women interpret innocent remarks or acts as being sexist). On the other hand, benevolent sexism represents evaluations of women that may appear positive (e.g., women should be cherished and protected by men), yet actually have lasting negative effects for gender equality.

I found that once the data is disaggregated by gender and race, white women's political behavior proves very different than women of color. Among white women, ambivalent sexist views positively and significantly predict vote choice for Trump, controlling for all other factors. However, for women of color, this relationship was negative and posed no statistically significant relationship to voting for Trump. Women and men of all backgrounds can hold both gender and racial based prejudices about one another and internally (Jackman 1994). To understand the extent to which such views influence political behaviors and the variation between white women and women of color we must move beyond the monolithic partisan gender gap narrative in American presidential politics.

Arguably, the brunch group of black women intrinsically understood that white women, given their position as "second in sex, but first in race," could be the only majority group of female voters to choose Trump's proffered "velvet glove" over the extended hand of a white woman running for US president. Women of color being second in both sex and race are rarely able to disentangle the impact of their race, gender and other identities on their decision-making (Collins 1990; Gay and Tate 1998; Hooks 1981, 1984; Jordan-Zachery 2007; King 1988; Prestage 1977).

It is useful to confront *why* intergroup dialogue about race and the gender gap in politics is so difficult and is rarely held in so-called mixed company between women of color and white women. In the Trump era of heightened racial polarization, such conversations in "mixed company" both inside and outside of academia can be mentally exhausting, particularly for women of color who may often battle daily racialized and gendered microaggressions. Such honest conversations in "mixed company" *between* women of different racial, ethnic, and cultural backgrounds can be productive. However, for women of color, "racesplaining fatigue" (often about the legacies of white privilege), coupled with inequitable power dynamics, can make engaging in such open dialogue draining and costly in the workplace as well as in social circles. It is also important that such honest dialogue takes place *among* white women and between white women and men to advance the nation's conversation about race, gender, and politics. Ignoring the issues that stand between our dialogue, including persistence of sexism, racism, and inequality, do not make them go away. However, a lack of discourse stands in the way of the prospects for coalition-building toward the road ahead.

References

Azari, J. (2017), "What Hillary Clinton's Candidacy Meant for Women," Retrieved from https://www.vox.com/mischiefs-of-faction/2017/11/6/16610624/clinton-candidacy-women (November 7).

Bracic, A., M. Israel-Trummel and A. Shortle (2018), "Is Sexism for White People? Gender Stereotypes, Race, and the 2016 Presidential Election," *Political Behavior*, doi: https://doi.org/10.1007/s11109-018-9446-8.

Cassese, E. C., T. D. Barnes and R. P. Branton (2015), "Racializing Gender: Public Opinion at the Intersection," *Politics & Gender*, 11: 1–26. doi: 10.1017/S1743923X14000567.

Cathy, C. (2003), "A Portrait of Continuing Marginality: The Study of Women of Color in American Politics," In S. J. Carroll (ed.), *Women and American Politics: New Questions, New Directions*, Oxford: Oxford University Press.

Collins, P. H. (1990), *Black Feminist Thought: Knowledge, Consciousness, and the Politics of Empowerment*, Boston, MA: UnwinHyman.

Frasure-Yokley, L. (2018), "Choosing the Velvet Glove: Women Voters, Ambivalent Sexism, and Vote Choice in 2016," *Journal of Race, Ethnicity, and Politics*, 1–23. doi: https://doi.org/10.1017/rep.2017.35.

Gay, C. and K. Tate (1998), "Doubly Bound: The Impact of Gender and Race on the Politics of Black Women," *Political Psychology*, 19 (1): 169–84.

Glick, P. and S. T. Fiske (1996), "The Ambivalent Sexism Inventory: Differentiating Hostile and Benevolent Sexism," *Journal of Personality and Social Psychology*, 70 (3): 491–512.

Glick, P. and S. T. Fiske (1997), "Hostile and Benevolent Sexism Measuring Ambivalent Sexist Attitudes Toward Women," *Psychology of Women Quarterly*, 31 (5): 119–35.

Glick, P. and S. T. Fiske (2001), "An Ambivalent Alliance: Hostile and Benevolent Sexism as Complementary Justifications for Gender Inequality," *American Psychologist*, 56 (2): 109–18.

Hooks, B. (1981), *Ain't I a Woman: Black Women and Feminism*, Boston, MA: South End Press.

Hooks, B. (1984), *Feminist Theory from Margin to Center*, Boston, MA: South End Press.

Jackman, Mary. (1994), *The Velvet Glove: Paternalism and Conflict in Gender, Class, and Race Relations*, Berkeley, CA: University of California Press.

Jordan-Zachery, J. S. (2007), "Am I a Black Woman or a Woman Who Is Black? A Few Thoughts on the Meaning of Intersectionality," *Politics & Gender*, 3 (2): 254–63.

Junn, J. (2016), "Hiding in Plain Sight: White Women Vote Republican," Retrieved from http://politicsofcolor.com/white-women-vote-republican/.

King, D. K. (1988), "Multiple Jeopardy, Multiple Consciousness: The Context of a Black Feminist Ideology," *Signs*, 14 (1): 42–72.

Prestage, J. L. (1977), "Black Women State Legislators: A Profile," *A Portrait of Marginality: The Political Behavior of the African Woman*, 31 (5): 400–18.

Roberts, L. M. and R. J. Ely (2016), "Why Did So Many White Women Vote for Donald Trump?," Retrieved from http://fortune.com/2016/11/17/donald-trump-women-voters-election/.

Rogers, K. (2016), "White Women Helped Elect Donald Trump," Retrieved from https://www.nytimes.com/2016/12/01/us/politics/white-women-helped-elect-donald-trump.html?_r=0.

Ruiz-Grossman, S. (2016), "Dear Fellow White Women: We F**ked This Up," Retrieved from http://www.huffingtonpost.com/entry/dear-white-women-we-messed-this-up-election-2016_us_582341c9e4b0aac62488970e.

Smooth, W. (2006), "Intersectionality in Electoral Politics: A Mess Worth Making," *Politics & Gender*, 2 (03): 400–14. doi: 10.1017/S1743923X06261087.

Tien, C. (2017), "The Racial Gap in Voting Among Women: White Women, Racial Resentment, and Support for Trump," *New Political Science*, doi: 10.1080/07393148.2017.1378296.

22

The Year After

A'shanti F. Gholar

No one can deny that Secretary Clinton's run for office was inspiring. I got to watch the 2016 presidential election from the point of view of the National Political Director for Emerge, an organization that recruits and trains Democratic women to run for office. Throughout the year, when I read interviews of women candidates across the country discussing their campaigns, the majority of them mentioned how running at the same time as Hillary kept them motivated and made them push harder on the rough days of their races because they saw how hard she was fighting.

I knew regardless of whether Hillary won or lost, women of all backgrounds across the country would be stepping up to run for office and make change in their communities. What I did not expect, however, was for this number to be in the tens of thousands. After Hillary's loss women said, "If not Hillary, then who? Me. It has to be me."

At Emerge, the day after the election we were bombarded with emails, phone calls, and social media messages from women wanting to run for office, to become campaign staff for women running for office or to donate to women running for office. This was the Hillary Effect—women refusing to sit idly by as sexism, racism, homophobia, and xenophobia invaded the public discourse from the highest elected office in the United States. Like us in the Emerge network, these women knew that they were the answer, and they were motivated to do their part to ensure that women were front and center at getting our democracy back on track.

While the day after the 2016 election will be forever seared in my mind, so is what occurred in the year after. I tell people that 2017 was quite the whirlwind for me as I spent 90 percent of my time traveling around the country engaging with individuals and organizations that were committed to getting more women in elected office. Emerge saw a huge increase in women applying for our programs, with many Emerge affiliates doubling their class sizes or running multiple training programs. We expanded heavily into new states, with an emphasis on the South—an area that has been neglected (and wrongfully so) by many Democratic and progressive organizations. Our network grew with new volunteers from women, such as accountants and lawyers, that wanted to offer their services to women running for office.

While traveling, Emerge was not the only organization out there speaking to the importance of this work and the impact that Hillary was having. Many organizations already in the recruitment and training space were just as busy as we were. EMILY's List had started a new program, Run to Win, offering one-day trainings to women interested in running for office after over thousands of women reached out to them. Higher Heights for America, an organization dedicated to building black women's political power, offered online webinars for black women that wanted to get more politically engaged while the Collective PAC, which was started in the fall of 2016, launched the Black Campaign School to train the next generation of black political leaders. Latino Victory saw its efforts increase as well as they expanded their work on building the power of Latinos as candidates and donors. There was a lot of work to be done, and not one organization could meet all of the demand. This led to even more organizations being created to help harness the post-election energy.

Run for Something became the organization for millennials that wanted to run for office. In this day and age, the notion that women have to be asked to run for office seven times does not apply to the millennial women—they are not waiting to be asked (see Rep. Lauren Underwood, Rep. Abby Finkenauer and Rep. Alexandria Ocasio-Cortez as examples). First Ask came on the scene to recruit women to run for office by encouraging them to run and connecting them to organizations that would support them (I am proud to be on the advisory board for this organization). The Sister District Project puts a focus on state legislative races across the country, encouraging individuals to adopt a candidate's race to volunteer for, and donate to. The Arena Summit is the hub to convene, train and support the next generation of candidates and campaign staff.

While many were focused on 2018, others and I knew that 2017 was the real test. Is this energy real? Are people paying attention to their local elections and not waiting until 2020 to see change? Will the women candidates that dominated the primary season be victorious in the general? On Election Night 2017, the answer was a resounding "yes," and this was no clearer than in Virginia when looking at the women who were elected to the Virginia House of Delegates.

The investments that Emerge and other organizations made in Virginia paid off dividends. A dozen seats that were held by white Republican men in districts that Hillary won had flipped to Democratic women. However, it was not just any women, it was women from all walks of life. Emerge alum Danica Roem became the first open transgender woman elected to a state house in the country. Kathy Tran became the first Asian American woman elected to the Virginia House of Delegates while her Emerge sisters Hala Ayala and Elizabeth Guzman became the first Latinas. Jennifer Carroll Foy defied the odds by not only winning the recount in her primary election but also giving birth to twins while running for office in the general election and joining the ranks of progressive prosecutors being elected to office.

The women who were inspired by Hillary in 2016 to run for office are now the role models for women who wanted to get politically engaged. In 2018, more women stepped up to run—and won. We now have over 100 women serving in Congress. Women now occupy 27 percent of state legislative seats. More women were elected to state-wide office from governor to secretary of state to attorney general. Women, especially black women, dominated mayoral elections of major cities. City councils, school boards, and county commissions now have more women sitting at the dais.

There are 520,000 elected offices in this country. Women are 51 percent of the population. We are far from holding 51 percent of elected offices in this country, but it can be done. Thanks to Hillary, each year we get closer, and this will be her everlasting effect on changing the face of politics in America. Thank you, Hillary.

23

Running because of Hillary

Denise S. Davis

In 1996, I was twelve years old when I first saw Hillary Clinton speak at UNLV. We were handed note cards to write down our questions for Hillary when we walked in. During the Q & A, I suddenly heard her say my name and read my question aloud. I quickly jumped to the edge of my seat in the middle of this large auditorium, as I didn't want to miss a single word of what would come next. "Hillary Clinton said MY name. She answered MY question!" was all I could think. I went home that night and wrote in my journal in all caps: "THIS WAS THE BEST NIGHT OF MY LIFE THAT I CAN REMEMBER."

A few weeks later, I experienced another highlight of my childhood as I received a letter in the mail from the White House. For a school assignment, we were asked to choose someone to write a letter to, and naturally, I chose to write to Hillary. Receiving a letter back from the First Lady whom I admired so much meant a lot. My dad, who laminated all important documents from my report cards to my sports certificates, had something new to add to the collection. The letter on White House stationary included these lines, "Dear Denise, Thank you for your thoughtful letter. I enjoy receiving letters from young people. . . . I am happy that you wrote to share your thoughts with me. It is important that young people feel involved in our government. I hope that as you grow up, you continue to share your opinions. Sincerely yours, Hillary Rodham Clinton."

My childhood impression of Hillary Clinton remains congruent with my impression now that I'm in my thirties. She's consistently been an unapologetically strong, resilient, smart woman who is a trailblazer. From taking on policy, instead of "baking cookies" as the First Lady to running to become the first female President—she has shown me all of my life that it is worth it to strive for more, and that "women's rights" are indeed "human rights." The fact that she encouraged young girls like me to "share your opinions" was one of the reasons why I was so drawn to her. She represented an empowered version of a woman that I seldom saw in the media during my childhood.

During the news coverage of the 2016 election and at the point when Donald Trump was declared the winner, my aunt texted me from Las Vegas and said, "I have never felt so insignificant as a woman." This sentiment was widely felt across the nation, and was simultaneously heartbreaking and infuriating. As someone who works full-time running a Women's Resource Center and teaching Women's and Gender Studies, I was especially impacted by the weight of this moment. It was a visceral reminder for all women that we indeed haven't made as much social progress as we might have thought. Because of this, I spent much of 2017 and the entirety of 2018 responding to what happened on the evening of November 8, 2016.

On the morning after the election, I turned on the television to watch Hillary Clinton's concession speech. I had tears flowing down my face, and I listened as closely as I could while still trying to process my shock and devastation from the night before. My beloved cat, Billary, was pawing at the Hillary Clinton cardboard cut-out still in the living room from the Election Night party. At some point in Hillary's speech, as she encouraged young women to not give up and to stay engaged in politics, I had an overwhelming feeling come across me. I thought, "Oh wow. I have to run for office now." This was not the plan. The plan was to work as hard as I could to help elect Hillary Clinton, who would be our first female president. My mind was still spinning at the inevitability of Clinton's victory and the stunning reality that it did not happen. "I have to run for office." This was not the plan, but now it seemed that it had to be.

I have spent most of my adult life living in Redlands, California, a town I fell in love with during my time here as a college student. Redlands has been historically a very conservative city. During the 2016 election, I knew I was going to be met with mixed reactions when I decided to initiate the "Redlands for Hillary" campaign. In addition to organizing volunteers to do weekly phone banking, I would wear Hillary t-shirts and hats around town. Like many Hillary supporters, I felt frustrated by the fact that deciding to show public support for HRC was often a very brave thing do to. Republicans would often give dirty looks, and the Bernie supporters would frequently try to engage in arguments. However, something very valuable happened for me while going around town in the Hillary attire. People started coming out of the woodwork—coming up to me and whispering, "I like your shirt. I'm supporting her!" I didn't know it at the time, but these moments of finding like-minded people in Redlands would eventually build up enough to convince me that it wasn't an impossible idea to think I could run for office—and win.

I approached my campaign for the Redlands City Council in a way that I watched Hillary do for years—I did my homework. I prepared as much as humanly possible. I had meetings upon meetings with elected officials, community activists and organizers, local organizations and everyone imaginable in an attempt to build a base of awareness and support. I applied for and was accepted into the Emerge California training program, which was an amazing resource for me as I learned the nuts and bolts of campaigning while building my network of incredible women who would be there to support each other through the whole process. Most importantly, I made sure that people knew why I was doing this—to bring forth my talents and passions to serve a city I deeply care about, while also highlighting the important need to diversify the dais.

My campaign, while on a much smaller scale, had some parallels with Hillary's. While she was working hard to become the first female president, I was working to become the first openly LGBTQ Council Member in Redlands. The uphill battle of helping people to envision something that's never existed before took tireless amounts of effort, explanation, and education. The campaign took me out of my comfort zone every single day. It was one of the hardest things I've ever done, but also one of the most rewarding. I was surrounded by so many people who, like me, were working desperately to produce a result on Election Day 2018 that would be different from what we went through in 2016. Our internal campaign slogan toward the end of the race was to "make sure we wake up with no regrets on the day after the election."

To my great relief, we ended up celebrating our successful campaign on November 6, 2018. We built a grassroots effort that mobilized hundreds of people to get involved. I won over four opponents, receiving over 51 percent of the total vote. Immediately upon being sworn in, my Council colleagues selected me to be the Mayor Pro Tem. I'm overjoyed about the opportunity to serve in this role, and for the learning and growing that's come as a result of this dive into the political arena. None of this would have happened without Hillary Clinton's influence and impact on my life. I am proud to be one of the undoubtedly many women and people from marginalized communities who ran because of Hillary. Her courage, grace, intelligence, and drive to keep going has inspired confidence in so many of us—a profoundly personal gift that will have lasting public impact for generations to come.

Stronger Together

How Hillary Clinton May Have Nudged More Women to Run for Office

Kristin Kanthak

Researchers interested in the large and persistent gender gap[1] in elected officials know that one of the main reasons there are so few women in office is that so few women run. For those of us who study women's political ambition, then, the question of the effect of Clinton's run in 2016 on the political ambition of women was vitally important. Did seeing Hillary Clinton run for office make women more likely to be willing to run themselves?

Just before the 2016 election, my colleague Chris Bonneau and I conducted an experiment to try to answer that question. In our experiment, we showed participants short online campaign ads that had been created by Clinton's campaign team. In some of the ads, Clinton was giving a speech at a large rally. In others, she was listening carefully as supporters told her about the issues that meant the most to them. We wanted to see what the effect was of seeing Hillary Clinton in different contexts, and had some hunches about how women would react. When watching the first ad, maybe women would be more averse to running for office because they did not want to give angry speeches about how they were ready to fight. In watching the second, maybe they would be more interested in politics if they saw that campaigning was also about a lot of compassionate listening to people whose problems you can help solve. Were women more likely to express interest in running for political office after having seen her in this more non-traditional campaign activity?

It turned out that we were wrong. Seeing Clinton in these non-traditional campaign situations did not increase women's political ambition. Indeed, there was really only one thing that mattered: what they thought about Hillary Clinton herself. When we showed women who liked Hillary Clinton a campaign ad featuring Hillary Clinton, they were slightly more likely to indicate they would be willing to run for office than were those who were in a group that saw an unrelated ad. For those women who were neutral or disliked Clinton, viewing the ad had no effect.

Here's how the experiment worked: we asked our participants a series of questions about a variety of topics, some having to do with politics ("How warmly do you feel about Hillary Clinton?") and some not ("How warmly do you feel about bicyclists?"). Then we showed them one of five randomly assigned short videos. Four were pro-Clinton campaign ads and the fifth—the "control" video—was an unrelated video about a bicycle borrowing program. We then asked participants another set of questions. One of those questions asked them how likely they thought they were to run for office someday. Because we randomly assigned subjects to videos, we can assume that the groups are essentially similar on all dimensions other than what video they saw. When we see differences in the groups, then, we can attribute those differences to the effect of the video.

Can we know exactly how many women Hillary Clinton inspired to run for office? Of course not. Human behavior is generally too complicated, and women remain unlikely to run. We are talking about very small numbers. In our study, the effect of seeing a Hillary Clinton ad made women's probability of saying they were likely to run for office increase from a dismal 0.01 probability to only a slightly less dismal 0.03 probability. Seeing Hillary Clinton run, then, does not instantly turn individuals who would never run for office into future candidates who are replete with political ambition. But this is a big country. If you can imagine that just one hundredth of the approximately 160 million women in the United States were fans of Hillary Clinton, and seeing Clinton in a campaign ad increases the probability of a woman running for office by 0.02, then using the mathematics of expected value indicates that her historic run for office may be responsible for as many as 32,000 more new women candidates in the years to come.

But willingness to run is not the only effect Hillary Clinton's run had on women's involvement in politics. In another research project, I am drawing on a team of undergraduate researchers to use Federal Elections Commission[2] data and track down information on the more than 450,000 individual contributors to Clinton's presidential campaign. Just under 30 percent of Clinton's contributors were women making a donation to a candidate's campaign for the first time. That translates to just under 140,000 women who had never picked up a pen and written a cheque to a candidate before Clinton ran, but now they have. What will happen to these women in the future? Will they keep contributing to candidates?

Will they participate in other ways? Will they end up deciding to run for office themselves?

A great many women—some included in other chapters this volume—explicitly give Hillary Clinton credit for sparking their personal political ambition. The stories these individuals share about their own experiences are vital to our understanding of the long-term effects of Hillary Clinton's run. We know Hillary Clinton's run for office matters because a great many women told us their stories about why she mattered to them.

At the same time, one of the benefits of large social scientific studies like the ones I discuss here is that we can better understand the Hillary Effect in the public at large. In our experimental study, fans of Hillary Clinton experienced a small increase in their political ambition when compared to a control group. We asked the subjects a wide range of questions after they viewed the ad, only one of which was about political ambition. Most of our subjects likely had no idea that seeing Hillary Clinton run for office made them slightly more likely to run themselves. Similarly, women who donated for the first time to Hillary Clinton's campaign likely saw themselves merely giving to a candidate they liked. Few of them were probably aware that most people don't donate, and that donating once might prompt them to donate again—or to remain involved in politics in other ways. These data indicate that the Hillary Effect on women's political ambition could be perhaps small for any particular woman, while still being large indeed when these small effects are amortized over all of the women who might have been affected.

Furthermore, it may be difficult for individual women to disentangle the hope they felt from Clinton's campaign from the anger they felt from Trump's subsequent victory. Memory is a notoriously tricky thing. But these large-scale studies I report here indicate that we perhaps ought to believe them when women report a Hillary Effect rather than a Trump effect. In both the large-scale studies I discuss here, the effects are based on responses to Clinton's run, not on Trump's victory. Reactions to Clinton's political ads and decisions to contribute to Clinton's campaign occurred before Donald Trump's historic victory had occurred—and indeed occurred when a great many people felt Clinton's victory was inevitable. Anger from that victory may have added fuel to the fire and prompted women to run in historic numbers in 2018 and beyond. But the research I outline here demonstrates that Clinton herself almost certainly had something to do with how that fire got lit in the first place.

Part Four

"Our Children Are Watching": Clinton's Impact on Parents and Kids

Preface

Jennifer L. Merolla

I wish she [Clinton's mother] could have seen the America we're going to build together. An America, where if you do your part, you reap the rewards. Where we don't leave anyone out, or anyone behind. An America where a father can tell his daughter: yes, you can be anything you want to be. Even President of the United States.

—Hillary Clinton[1]

These were the closing lines to Hillary Clinton's full announcement speech delivered to a large crowd in New York in June of 2015. The odds this time around seemed better than in 2008, making the historic nature of her run all the more salient. In her memoir *What Happened*, Clinton (2017) reflects on how throughout the campaign, she thought it important to recognize the weight of the moment for women and girls. Not only would her election result in the first woman president of the United States, but it would also likely have downstream effects in sending a strong message to parents and children that there are no bounds to a young girl's aspirations.

The enthusiasm around Clinton's historic candidacy grew even more as the general election rolled around. On Halloween, images of young girls dressed as Clinton made their rounds on social media. On Election Day, mothers and daughters dressed in suffragette white or sported a pants suit. People placed "I voted" stickers on the graves of the suffragettes. At least for much of that day, there was a strong sense that anything was possible. And while Clinton did not break that hardest, highest glass ceiling, the contributions in Part 4, all authored by political scientists, attest to how her presence in the race, and her response to her loss, have had important consequences on young children, adolescents, mothers, and fathers.

Given the underrepresentation of women in political life, it is likely not a surprise to learn that there is limited scholarly work that has examined the significance of women role models in politics for children. In one of the earliest studies on this topic Campbell and Wolbrecht (2006) found that when women political leaders attain greater national visibility through the media, girls participate in political discussions more often and are more likely to report higher levels of future political involvement. In a follow-up to that study using panel data Wolbrecht and Campbell (2017) find that this effect is especially likely when a woman candidate is new and has a good chance of winning. Similar findings have emerged from research that has considered the impact of women candidates on college students (Greenlee, Holman, and VanSickle-Ward 2014). Much of the work to date has focused on the congressional level, given the lack of viable women candidates at the presidential level. Furthermore, the focus has largely been on older girls, those in middle school, high school, and college.

The contributions in Part 4 probe the meaning of Clinton's historic candidacy for president across multiple groups and multiple dimensions. In a piece originally published in the *Monkey Cage* during the election (and updated in this part), Wolbrecht and Campbell argue that their earlier research on role models suggests that seeing Clinton run for president will likely increase political engagement among young women, given that she was the first viable woman to run for a major party in the general election, and given that she often highlighted being a role model.

The other contributions pick up where Wolbrecht and Campbell leave off, in terms of reflections on personal experience and in academic research. In "Hillary Clinton, my daughter, and me," Abby K. Wood reflects on the importance of having such a prominent woman role model, and how the election gave her hope that she could point to "Madam President" and say to her daughter, "See? You can be *anything*." Even though Clinton did not win, she witnessed how seeing Clinton on the campaign trail shaped her young daughter's expectations about women in government in ways she hadn't anticipated.

Also in this part, we learn about an ambitious research program being led by Jill S. Greenlee, Angela Bos, Mirya Holman, Celeste Lay, and Zoe Oxley. The team surveyed and interviewed over 1,500 elementary school kids after the 2016 election. Their aim was to document and better understand what children think about political leaders and politics after such an historic election. A vast majority of children knew that a woman had never held the presidency and that Clinton was running for office. Furthermore, more than twice as many children thought Clinton would do a better job in office than Trump, and this did not vary between boys and girls, a finding that is somewhat surprising, especially considering gender dynamics in elementary school! One of the interesting innovative exercises the group asked the children to do was to draw pictures of political leaders. While the vast majority of pictures featured male leaders, of those that included images of women, most were of Clinton.

After reading about young children, the contributions shift to mothers of older daughters. In "Real moms of Palo Alto, real takeaways from Hillary's candidacy," Melissa Michelson shares findings from focus groups she conducted with mothers. She notes that many of her participants were inspired by Clinton's candidacy and thought it was important to share the historic moment with their daughters. Clinton's loss and reaction to that loss gave them a new sense of the importance of doing more than voting and inspired them to become more involved. The moms also reflected on how Hillary's candidacy had inspired their daughters to be more politically interested and active, including paying attention to the news and getting involved at their local schools.

After discussing the impact of Clinton on children and on mothers, we turn to the contribution by Jill S. Greenlee, Tatishe Nteta, Libby Sharrow, and Jesse H. Rhodes, who examine how Clinton's run for office impacted fathers. They begin by noting that Clinton often highlighted the symbolic importance of her election for women and girls, like the quote at the beginning of this preface, in part to appeal to male listeners, especially fathers. Using original survey data, they find that fathers of first daughters, in both parties, were significantly more likely to support Clinton than fathers of first sons. Moreover, this dynamic persists when considering hypothetical candidates with a "Clintonesque message" on gender equality—having a first daughter led men to be more supportive of candidates who advocate for policies that advance women's well-being.

Clinton's run for office also impacted sons. Here, I will take the liberty of being one of the editors of this volume to reflect on this in my own household, as I am the parent of a young boy. My son was in kindergarten during the presidential primary. Even though he was young, given my goal of raising a feminist son,[2] we would have conversations about the election, about Clinton's historic run for office and of how underrepresented women are in government. It became clear to me the next election cycle how much those conversations and Clinton's run for office impacted him.

Since 2011, the local town where I live had a city council made up solely of men. Finally, during the 2018 cycle, a woman who had been very involved in the community and who grew up in the town decided to throw her hat into the ring. My son (now eight) and I again had conversations, this time about the local election, and he kept pressing me about whether I was going to vote for the woman running for office and thought we should get a sign in our yard to support her candidacy. When I asked him why he wanted me to support the only woman in the race, he didn't say because there aren't any women on the council, but remarked that she cares about the community and has the best understanding of it.

Fast-forward a few weeks, and my son was interviewing the councilwoman-elect for a class project on local government. During the interview he learned that our city is shifting from an at-large to a district-based system in the next election cycle, to which he replied that I should run for office since I am highly qualified. While my preference is to study politics, rather than practice it, my son's comment made me realize just how much he has been affected by our discussions about women's underrepresentation and by seeing strong, qualified, caring, and confident women run for political office. It may be that we would have had conversations about the underrepresentation of women in government even if Clinton had not run in 2016, but I tend to think that her run opened up a space for conversations that don't always occur to us to have. And, seeing her on the campaign trail means that he envisions a politics that is more inclusive of women.

References

Campbell, D. E. and C. Wolbrecht (2006), "See Jane Run: Women Politicians as Role Models for Adolescents," *The Journal of Politics*, 68 (2): 233–47.

Clinton, H. R. (2017), *What Happened?*, New York: Simon & Schuster.

Greenlee, J. S., M. R. Holman and R. VanSickle-Ward (2014), "Making It Personal: Assessing the Impact of In-Class Exercises on Closing the Gender Gap in Political Ambition," *Journal of Political Science Education*, 10 (1): 48–61.

Wolbrecht, C. and D. E. Campbell (2017), "Role Models Revisited: Youth, Novelty, and the Impact of Female Candidates," *Politics, Groups, & Identities*, 5 (3): 418–34.

Even in Defeat, Clinton's Campaign Could Still Inspire Young Women

Christina Wolbrecht and David Campbell

Hillary Clinton's bid to become the first female president ended on Election Night 2016.[*] But even in defeat, she sought in her concession speech[1] to inspire and encourage young women who had invested hope in her campaign: "And to all the little girls who are watching this, never doubt that you are valuable and powerful and deserving of every chance and opportunity in the world to pursue and achieve your own dreams."

Clinton's loss is no doubt a setback for the efforts to shatter the "highest and hardest glass ceiling" in American politics, but our research suggests that her campaign may still increase young women's political engagement. What Clinton's candidacy ultimately means for women's underrepresentation in office, however, is less clear.

One reason Clinton's campaign may spur female political engagement is that Clinton herself sought to cultivate an image as a role model. When Clinton secured[2] the Democratic nomination in July, she tweeted[3] a picture of herself dancing with a young girl. "To every little girl who dreams big: Yes, you can be anything you want—even president," she wrote. "This night is for you."

We find that adolescent girls become more likely to say they plan to be active in politics as adults when the number of women running competitive campaigns for office—not just winning—increases (Campbell and Wolbrecht 2006). Given that Clinton won the popular vote and lost the Electoral College by a relatively small margin, we can surely describe her candidacy as competitive.

But such effects are not automatic. There are at least two factors that affect whether female candidates end up serving as political role models for young

---

[*] This article was first published on the Monkey Cage on 14 November 2016. This version has been slightly revised.

women: how women in politics are described by the media, and whether politics are discussed over the dinner table as a result.

First, adolescent girls are more likely to become interested in political activism when the media characterizes female politicians as unusual, pathbreaking, or remarkable. It seems a pretty safe bet that Clinton's campaign has been viewed as pathbreaking by most Americans.

Headlines from the Democratic National Convention typically noted[4] that she was the first woman at the top of a major-party ticket. In her acceptance speech,[5] Clinton called her nomination a "milestone in our nation's march toward a more perfect union."

Moreover, Donald Trump ensured that gender remained front and center during the campaign. By claiming that Clinton's appeal was based on her playing the "woman card"[6] and calling her a "nasty woman" during the final debate, Trump helped remind Americans that she was attempting to make history.

Second, we find that it's not just what girls see or read that matters. It may also depend on whether the Clinton campaign spurred conversations about politics between parents and daughters at home.

When the presence of female politicians leads parents and children to talk politics, girls become more interested in political participation. Thus, parents play an important role in ensuring that youth make the connection between the political world and their own lives.

Ironically, this means that even the disparaging rhetoric about Clinton that arose[7] from Trump rallies and some of his supporters may help to engage young girls. If the unprecedented nature of Clinton's candidacy—highlighted by the candidate herself, her opponent, and the media—means politics became a topic of conversation within America's homes, adolescent girls may become more engaged in politics as a result.

Over the long run, the reverberations could be significant. If the political engagement of young women increases, that may help undermine one of the key reasons for women's underrepresentation: women are far less likely to run for office than men (Lawless and Fox 2010). Seeing a female candidate run for president may lead more girls and women to envision themselves as candidates as well—the record number of women who ran in the 2018 midterms suggests that this has already begun.

Of course, there are reasons to doubt that Clinton's unsuccessful bid will lead more women to politics. Concerns about discrimination help explain the reluctance of qualified women to seek elective office (Fox and Lawless 2011). And although gender bias—by the media and voters—is far less prevalent

(Hayes and Lawless 2015) in politics than it used to be, it is clear that a woman running for office exposes herself to considerable scrutiny and criticism. To the extent that the gender-based attacks on Clinton becomes the lesson[8] pundits draw from the 2016 race, it may serve to discourage more women from running (Hayes and Lawless 2016).

But ultimately, whether a "Hillary generation" of politically engaged young women emerges to pick up the pieces will certainly shape the course of women's representation in the United States for years to come.

References

Campbell, D. E. and C. Wolbrecht (2006), "See Jane Run: Women Politicians as Role Models for Adolescents," *The Journal of Politics*, 68 (2): 233–47.

Fox, R. L. and J. L. Lawless (2011), "Gendered Perceptions and Political Candidacies: A Central Barrier to Women's Equality in Electoral Politics," *American Journal of Political Science*, 55 (1): 59–73.

Hayes, D. and J. L. Lawless (2015), "A Non-Gendered Lense? Media, Voters, and Female Candidates in Contemporary Congressional Elections," *Perspectives on Politics*, 13 (March): 95–118.

Lawless, J. L. and R. L. Fox (2010), *It Still Takes a Candidate: Why Women Don't Run for Office*, Cambridge: Cambridge University Press.

Hillary Clinton, My Daughter, and Me

Abby K. Wood

My parents told me over and over that I could be anything I wanted to be. I remember asking, after a long list of other career possibilities, "can I be president?" And hearing "yes, you can." Their words were powerful, but they had very few role models to point to in order to assure me that my dreams could be reality. I'm a child of the 1980s, which means that I experienced many firsts for women as I grew up. I remember when Madeline Albright became Secretary of State, Elizabeth Dole ran for president, Lynette Woodard joined the Harlem Globetrotters, Sally Ride went to space, the WNBA was formed and Ann Richards became governor of Texas. But seeing a woman reach the highest office in the land was a dream. Americans weren't "ready" for a female president, the pollsters told us, betraying their opinion on the matter by asking the question in the first place.

For each of the key moments in which a role model or new avenue for women emerged, there have been far more moments in my life during which there was no woman to point to. Where were the pastors? The bishops? The superintendents? The police chiefs? The mayors? The generals? The CEOs? There were few to point to until I graduated from college, and even now, women make up a small minority of people holding these jobs.

If I had my experience as a child of the 1980s, what must Hillary's experience have been like? She came up before Madeline, before Elizabeth, before Title IX (and yes, before the WNBA). She had even fewer women in public life to point to as she shaped her political career. And, as I explain here, I believe that her candidacy is more important for our daughters than many of us realized at the time.

As spring turned to summer in 2016, my enthusiasm for Hillary fully blossomed. The thing I'd wanted for so long, a woman in the White House, was finally going to happen! A new form of equality! A new possibility! I would be able to point to "Madam President" and say to my daughter, "See? You can be *anything*." My eagerness to support Hillary was contagious, and my then three-year-old daughter, Beatrix, caught the bug. She met Hillary at a rally, learned the words to Fight Song and ogled all the campaign swag I bought, especially the cross-stitched pillow declaring: "A woman's place is in the White House." Beatrix's enthusiasm met mine, and it thrilled me.

One night during the Democratic Convention, we let her stay up late to watch President Obama give his speech about Hillary and the future of the party. Before President Obama took the stage, the convention showed a video about his presidency. Beatrix turned to me, sleepy in her footy pyjamas, and said two things that struck me to my core. As the first images of President Obama came on the screen, my daughter turned to me and said, "Mama, the president is a boy. Isn't that funny?" That President Obama is a "boy" struck her as "funny." She just assumed that woman presidents are a normal thing, and that having a man in the role was an exception to the rule. I smiled, and I hesitated. Should I explain the history of our country? That actually, US presidents have always been "boys," and this moment was historic and important because it had the potential to change who and what we see as powerful? Won't there be time for that later? Won't she learn, soon enough, of how unequal things have been for people who share her gender?

I chose to say nothing, and we returned to the video. As it ran, the screen filled with the now-famous shot of the war room, when President Obama and his advisers waited for news about whether the mission to "bring Bin Laden to justice" succeeded. In the image, Hillary sits between Robert Gates and Dennis McDonough in the foreground. Aside from a woman standing in the back of the room, Hillary is the only woman in the picture. As the shot panned, my daughter asked me, "Mama, why is it all boys in the room?" She hadn't seen Hillary.

This was a stark moment. I have seen that picture for years, and my main thought upon seeing Hillary is that she's awesome to have a seat at the table. I had never asked, "Where are the women?" as my daughter demanded. I am accustomed to being the only woman on the panel, the only woman on the committee, the only female co-author. For most of my life and most of my career, I have looked out and seen rooms full of men—even when I was among them as their equal. My daughter sees me in leadership roles, yes, but she also saw a woman campaign for the highest office in the land. Watching Hillary in debates, in speeches, and in person, commanding the room with authority and enthusiasm shaped my daughter's expectations about women in ways I hadn't anticipated. She expects much more gender balance than I do.

Social science backs up these experiences, aggregating these stories into actual statistical patterns, and demonstrating the link between descriptive representation and the role model effect. When women and girls see women in office, it can shape their political outlook. Watching women in office, we see new possibilities for ourselves (Mansbridge 1999; Wolbrecht and Campbell 2007). We gain interest in politics, perhaps because women candidates tend to discuss political issues that are relevant to us (Burns, Schlozman, and Verba 2001; Fridkin and Kenney 2014). We also discuss politics more when women are on the ballot (Campbell and Wolbrecht 2006; Wolbrecht and Campbell 2017). All of this matters for women's political engagement, girls' future plans and our vision of what is possible.

That's the story of Hillary Clinton, my daughter, and me. Through my daughter's elevated expectations, my own assumptions about who belongs in the room and who deserves to hold power have shifted too. Thank you, Hillary.

References

Burns, N., K. L. Schlozman, and S. Verba (2001), *The Private Roots of Public Action: Gender, Equality, and Political Participation*, Cambridge: Harvard University Press.

Campbell, D. and C. Wolbrecht (2006), "See Jane Run: Women Politicians as Role Models for Adolescents," *Journal of Politics*, 68 (2): 233–47.

Fridkin, K. L. and P. J. Kenney (2014), "How the Gender of U.S. Senators Influences People's Understanding and Engagement in Politics," *Journal of Politics*, 76 (4): 1017–31.

Mansbridge, J. (1999), "Should Blacks Represent Blacks and Women Represent Women? A Contingent 'Yes,'" *Journal of Politics*, 61 (3): 628–57.

Wolbrecht, C. and D. Campbell (2007), "Leading by Example: Female Members of Parliament as Political Role Models," *American Journal of Political Science*, 51 (3): 921–39.

Wolbrecht, C. and D. E. Campbell (2017), "Role models revisited: Youth, novelty, and the impact of female candidates," *Politics, Groups, and Identities*, 5 (3): 418–34.

Drawing Madam President

How Children Imagine Hillary Clinton as a Political Leader

Jill S. Greenlee, Angela L. Bos, Mirya R. Holman,
J. Celeste Lay, and Zoe M. Oxley

During the 2016 presidential election, images of young girls cheering at Hillary Clinton rallies, meeting the candidate herself and posing proudly in pantsuits were ubiquitous. These pictures conveyed a level of enthusiasm for Clinton that suggested her candidacy had a significant and positive impact on the political engagement of young girls. But these images were a curated snapshot of that political moment and can tell us less about the more nuanced ways that Clinton's candidacy may have shaped children's perceptions of politics and political leaders. Fortunately, our research begins to address some of these topics.

In the fall of 2017 and early months of 2018, we went to eighteen elementary and middle schools at four locations around the United States (greater Boston, upstate New York, northeastern Ohio and New Orleans). We interviewed and surveyed 1,545 children in grades 1–6. Our overarching aim was to document and better understand what children think about political leaders and politics. It was the year after the 2016 election, and while Hillary Clinton no longer served in public office as a First Lady, Senator or Secretary of State, we can glean from our data the impression that she had on these young children.

Our data suggest that Hillary Clinton's historic bid for the presidency may have had positive effects on levels of political awareness among children. Of the 446 children who were asked if they recognized the woman who ran as a major-party candidate for the presidency in 2016, 87 percent correctly identified Clinton; 90 percent of girls and 85 percent of boys recognized Clinton's image. In first grade only 74 percent could identify her, but by sixth grade, 97 percent could. When asked if a woman had ever been elected to the presidency, 82 percent of the 445 children who received this question correctly knew that the United States has never had a female president (85 percent of boys and 80 percent of girls). Thus, whereas boys were more likely to be aware that the president has always been male, girls were more likely to identify Clinton as a recent political candidate. Even more stark differences emerge by grade for this latter item: only 55 percent of first graders correctly answered that a woman has never sat in the White House, compared to 98 percent of sixth graders (and the percentage answering correctly increased for every grade). These descriptive findings suggest that Hillary Clinton's presidential bid had a meaningful effect on political awareness among these students, most especially the older children. They knew who she was, but they also knew that she (nor other women) had not yet occupied the highest office in the land.

How did these students evaluate Hillary Clinton? We asked a subset of 422 students what kind of job they think Clinton would have done, had she been elected to the presidency. Thirty percent said they thought she would have done a very good job; 28 percent thought she would have done a fairly good job; 9 percent not a very good job; and 25 percent thought she would have done a bad job (8 percent didn't know). Compare this to their evaluations of the current president, where 16 percent thought he is doing a very good job; 26 percent thought he is doing a fairly good job; 20 percent not a very good job; and 25 percent a bad job (12 percent said they did not know).[1] Note that nearly twice as many children felt that Clinton would have done a very good job as compared to the number of children who felt similarly about the current president. This is notable in part because generally women political leaders are seen as less competent than their male counterparts (Huddy and Terkildsen 1993). Moreover, looking at the data by gender, we find that boys and girls are quite similar with regard to their assessment of the type of president Hillary Clinton would have been.

Our study also allows us to draw more qualitative insights regarding how some children perceived Hillary Clinton through a unique measure we adapted from research in the STEM fields: the Draw a Political Leader Task. This measure is an open-ended task; children are asked to "imagine a political leader" and then draw what they imagined. After drawing, the children are asked to describe what they drew as well as discuss what their drawn leader is like and does on a typical day. Of the 1,404 drawings, 75 percent featured male leaders and 15 percent contained female leaders.[2] Most children drew non-specific characters, such as police officers or people working in an office or giving a speech; 538 (38 percent) drew known political leaders. Just over half (293) of the specific people were pictures of Donald Trump and only 41 (8 percent) of the known leaders were women. Of those, 37 percent were pictures of Hillary Clinton. Other female leaders drawn included Bree Newsome, Elizabeth Warren, Theresa May, Michele Obama and some local mayors. Perhaps not surprisingly, given the historical dominance of men in political leadership positions in the United States, of all male leaders drawn, 47 percent were known leaders as against the 19 percent of female leaders drawn that were known.

While few children drew Hillary Clinton, these pictures were overwhelmingly positive, suggesting that Clinton's candidacy had left a strong, positive impression on these young political observers. Students depicted Clinton as a caring and positive leader; in one case, she was wearing a rainbow pantsuit; in another she was smiling and giving a speech about why she should be president. They described her with words like kind and "jenurus" (generous), and said that as a political leader, she would work hard and make the world "awesome." In short, though few students drew Clinton, those that did overwhelmingly saw her as a positive force in politics.

Of the fifteen students who drew Hillary Clinton, eight were girls (four were boys, and two students did not report their gender). And almost all of these girls expressed an interest in engaging in the political world themselves. These findings fit with other work indicating that when women run for highly visible public offices, their candidacies lead to higher levels of self-reported interest in politics from young girls (Campbell and Wolbrecht 2006). Thus, our data suggest that part of Hillary Clinton's legacy may be that she helped some children see that while the United States has not yet elected a woman to the presidency, women are and can be powerful and positive political leaders. Even if the percentage of girls who are inspired later in life to run for office because of Hillary Clinton's candidacy increases only by a small amount, such a change could be consequential given the very low percentage of adults who do run for office. Yet it is also important to recognize that the majority of children sketched a man when asked to draw a political leader, suggesting that most children still see politics as a man's world. Indeed, it will likely take more time—and more female presidential nominees—for more children to be able to envision "Madam President" in her rainbow pantsuit doing good things in the world.

References

Campbell, D. E. and C. Wolbrecht (2006), "See Jane Run: Women Politicians as Role Models for Adolescents," *The Journal of Politics*, 68 (2): 233–24.

Huddy, L. and N. Terkildsen (1993), "Gender Stereotypes and the Perception of Male and Female Candidates," *American Journal of Political Science*, 37: 119–47.

28

Real Moms of Palo Alto, Real Takeaways from Hillary's Candidacy

Melissa R. Michelson

As a political science professor, I spend a considerable amount of time talking to other politics experts. As a mom, I spend a considerable amount of time talking to other moms in my community in Palo Alto, California. I've always valued the way those conversations help me break out of my academic bubble and see things from a different perspective.

These moms were inspired by Hillary's candidacy. Several attended fundraisers for Hillary, often bringing along their children. The moms of daughters especially thought it was important, despite the sticker shock of those events, to share the historic moment of Hillary's candidacy with their young girls. Other moms helped out by making get-out-the-vote phone calls to Democrats in swing states. Other women were less involved but had voted for Hillary. All of them thought until Election Night that she was sure to be the next president.

In the summer of 2018, I sat down for a series of three focus groups with those local moms (and in one, their fourteen-year-old daughter) to get a better sense of how they remembered and were affected by Hillary's candidacy.

The biggest effect was clearly a new sense of the importance of doing more than voting, to get more involved—as R put it, "It's not enough to just vote and write checks." It's easy, living in our neighborhood, to just ignore what's going on in politics; we live in a safe, comfortable bubble of upper-middle-class privilege. But these women were politicized and ready to invest their time and energy. They were more involved in their communities and in local organizations, thinking about the midterm 2018 elections and beyond.

To some extent, it was difficult for the moms to separate the legacy of Hillary's candidacy from the effect of Trump's administration. Much of their post-election activism, including attending marches and contacting their representatives, is meant to voice their opposition to Trump's policies and statements. But even this anti-Trump political behavior was evidence of how they had been impacted by Clinton, as illustrated by an exchange between J and her fourteen-year-old daughter E.

As E was sharing her participation in gun control advocacy at her high school, she choked up, saying, "The adults aren't doing anything, the kids organized the March for Our Lives. It's all so messed up." J comforted E with a hand on her shoulder.

J: That's the Hillary effect. She did her part. She ran for president. Now we have to do our part.

E: Trump is president and he's not using his power to fix anything. We have to use the power that we have, the power of the people.

J: It taught us that you do have that power.

Another takeaway for the moms was the sense that women need to be more united, despite socialization that trains us to tear down and criticize other women. Reflecting on Hillary's campaign, they saw that she was judged differently because she was a woman, and that media coverage of her hair, her clothes and so on, was unfairly harsh. This came up in all three groups. In the first, C commented: "Watching all she's went through has created a different level of awareness of what women go through. . . . Our awareness of sexism is increased and our tolerance for it has shortened." In another focus group, J commented (at first hesitantly): "Do you think part of it is that women are so hard on each other—that she didn't win? I think that." In another group, N offered that women have now come together as a sisterhood, rather than thinking they can only succeed by tearing down other women like crabs in a barrel. Now, N added, "there's a sense of community and values," and a common goal of the empowerment of women.

Also, in all three groups, the moms I talked to said Hillary's candidacy had inspired their daughters to be more politically interested and active, including paying attention to the news and getting involved at their local schools. D shared that her eleven-year-old daughter had run for president at school. "I think in some ways it's just her nature, but in some ways it was her being inspired because we had talked about the need for more women to run for office. . . . I think going to the [Hillary for President] event got her thinking about it." In another group, L shared that she had seen a similar effect on her eighteen-year-old daughter, R, during Hillary's first presidential run.

N: It's really inspiring. Y's only 9, so for her to watch and cheer Hillary on—here's a really powerfully woman—to say to her, here's an example of what you could do. Previously the idea of an American woman president wasn't even something on the checkbox.

L: I felt that the last time [in 2008]. R was younger, she was 9 or 10, she got to see that. Especially for girls like age 7–10, before middle school, that's the crucial time. So she was right at that age where she felt inspired by a strong woman running for president. So that encouraged my daughter—you can be a strong woman.

N: That was the first parlay into politics for my daughter. She had opinions. So here is my little kid who, she understood. At such a young age she was having exposure, her exposure to how important government is. . . . I don't remember thinking [that way] at nine. Now the definition of a president isn't a male president. Now it's androgynous.

The moms in my neighborhood have heard that more women are running for office because of Hillary's candidacy, and believe we will soon see a woman president. Her candidacy helped them realize how much it meant to them to see that happen.

E: Now there's a lot more women who are gonna run for president and that's pretty cool.

J: We were in Boston visiting gravestones, and I was thinking about, the day of the vote, people were taking their "I voted" stickers and putting them on the [graves of the] suffragettes. Women really wanted that. We can do it. Other countries broke the glass ceiling so many years before us.

E: People thought women wouldn't do it. Now women can actually do stuff.

J: She still broke the glass ceiling, just by being there.

All of the moms I talked to saw a future woman presidency as inevitable, and they saw many more women were running for office. They also thought that the next woman candidate would be more aware of the challenges they would face as a woman, able to learn from the 2016 campaign.

N: People are more interested in politics now and care more to get involved.

L: That's Trump.

N: No. Women are excited to participate. That's Hillary. Politics is a new frontier for us to conquer. You don't have to just be a secretary. [When I was growing up] you could be a nurse, you could be a teacher, now . . .

Now, a woman can be president. It's gonna happen.

29

Fatherhood, First Daughters, and the First Woman Presidential Candidate

Elizabeth A. Sharrow, Jesse H. Rhodes, Tatishe M. Nteta, and Jill S. Greenlee

On June 13, 2015, Hillary Clinton formally announced her campaign for the Democratic Party presidential nomination from the steps of Roosevelt Island in New York City. In her speech, Clinton spoke of the many challenges facing the United States both at home and abroad, as well as her plans to address these issues.

Given her long record of public service, it was no surprise that Clinton emphasized her experiences as a First Lady, Senator and Secretary of State as reasons to support her candidacy. Yet, Clinton also highlighted her gender—and the symbolic importance of her election for women and girls—to appeal to male listeners, especially fathers. Her election, Clinton claimed, would help build "an America where a father can tell his daughter: yes, you can be anything you want to be. Even President of the United States" (Frizell 2015). With these words, Clinton strongly suggested that fathers of daughters should carefully consider the interests of their female children in deciding how to cast their ballot in the 2016 presidential contest.

Was this strategy effective? Were fathers of daughters more likely to prefer Clinton in the 2016 presidential election compared to fathers of sons? And did Clinton's direct appeals to fathers of daughters influence their voting behavior?

Our research suggests that some voters—in particular, fathers whose first child is a girl—are indeed influenced by women candidates" claims that their election can advance the interest of young women and girls (Greenlee et al. 2018). Focusing on the 2016 election, we show that men whose first child is a girl, when compared to men whose first child was a boy, were (1) more likely to vote for Clinton on Election Day, and (2) more likely to support a fictional female congressional candidate who made a similar "Clintonesque" appeal to fathers of daughters.

We conclude that how women candidates construct campaign appeals matters. Female candidates who underscore the importance of their elections for the interests of women and girls are more likely to draw support from men with first daughters.

Research suggests that becoming a father has the potential to alter men's political attitudes and behaviors (Elder and Greene 2012). However, the gender of the first child matters, particularly when it comes to men's opinions about issues relating to gender and women's equality. Having a daughter as a first child may freshly awaken men to the many obstacles to gender equality that women and girls face and raise the salience of these matters in men's minds. Indeed, in our research, we found that the experience of "first daughterhood" leads men to become more supportive of policies that seek to advance gender equality (Sharrow et al. 2018). This stands in contrast to mothers' gender equality attitudes, which are not directly influenced by the gender of the first child. This is likely because women are already well acquainted with issues relating to gender equality prior to the arrival of a first daughter, and therefore are less affected by the gender of their eldest child.

Based on this research, we suspected that the experience of fathering an eldest daughter might also lead men to more strongly support women candidates for political office—especially if these candidates highlight the benefits of their candidacies for young women and girls.

To test this argument, we designed an original survey of 382 American fathers and 514 American mothers.[1] In our survey, we asked each parent in our sample about the gender and birth order of each of their children. We also asked whether they voted for Clinton in the 2016 general election. The survey also included questions about fathers' partisanship, ideology, education, age, religiosity, income employment status, marital status, evaluations of the economy, racial attitudes, and gender attitudes to account for other factors in our analyses that likely influenced support for Clinton.

Did fathers of first daughters, more so than fathers of first sons, support Clinton in the presidential election? Our results suggest that they did.

After controlling for the factors listed, we find that fathers of first daughters, relative to fathers of first sons, were ten percentage points more likely to vote for Clinton in 2016. Notably, this effect is also unique to fathers; we did *not* find that having a daughter as a first child influenced mothers' voting patterns. Most strikingly, having a first daughter has similar effects among Democratic and Republican fathers. Although the message was *more* appealing among Democrats than Republicans, the "first daughter effect" was present for fathers across the political spectrum.

While these results point to the effectiveness of this campaign strategy in mobilizing support among fathers of first daughters for Clinton in 2016, it remains unclear if such appeals can also be used by women candidates running for political office more generally. To assess whether other candidates can successfully use rhetorical appeals similar to those Clinton applied in her campaign, we also conducted an experiment. We randomly assigned our respondents to one of three different descriptions of a fictional female congressional candidate named "Molly Smith." In the first version, we briefly described Smith as a candidate running to become the first woman to represent Minnesota's fictional 10th District. In the second version, we added the information that Smith "supports policies that would help increase the participation of women in careers in science, technology, engineering, and mathematics."

In the final version, in addition to the information provided in version two, we included a quotation attributed to Smith, which was designed to mirror Clinton's appeal to fathers of daughters: "This campaign is about making sure there are no ceilings, no limits on any of us, and to ensure that our daughters will forever know that there is no barrier to who they are and what they can be in the United States of America." This design allowed us to test the more general impact of Clinton's *messaging* toward fathers and to investigate the symbolic importance of a woman candidate like Clinton on American fathers.

Once again, we find that fathers of first daughters, more so than fathers of first sons, were likely to support a congressional candidate when the candidate makes an appeal touting the importance of her candidacy for women and girls. For fathers with first daughters, being exposed to a message that mirrored Clinton's appeal increased the likelihood of support for our fictional women candidate by twenty-five percentage points when compared to fathers of first daughters who were told that the candidate would be the first woman to represent the district. Among fathers of first sons, exposure to the same Clintonesque message only increased the likelihood of support for the candidate by seven percentage points relative to fathers of first sons who were informed that the candidate would make history as the district's first women candidate. Again, we found this effect only among fathers, and not among mothers.

Together, the results from both studies suggest that Clinton's *message* mattered. Emphasizing the importance of her election for women and girls attracted support from fathers of first daughters in her campaign to become the first female president of the United States.

For complex reasons, Clinton fell short in her effort to make history in 2016. But her campaign provides valuable lessons for female candidates seeking to broaden the base of their political appeal. As more and more women run for Congress and other state-wide elections (CAWP 2018), female candidates seeking support from men should not only speak to their intentions to represent the interests of women and girls but also highlight the symbolic importance of their election for the daughters of American fathers. In doing this, they may tap into an unexpected source of electoral support.

References

Ansolabehere, S. and B. Schaffner (2016), "COOPERATIVE CONGRESSIONAL ELECTION STUDY, 2016: COMMON CONTENT," [Computer File] Release 2: August, 4 2017. Cambridge, MA: Harvard University [producer], http://cces.gov. harvard.edu.

CAWP, Center for American Women in Politics (2018), "By the Numbers: Women Congressional Candidates in 2018," *Center for American Women and Politics, Rutgers Eagleton Institute of Politics*, http://www.cawp.rutgers.edu/congressional-candidat es-summary-2018.

Elder, L. and S. Greene (2012), *The Politics of Parenthood*, Albany, NY: SUNY Press.

Frizell, S. (2015), "Read the Full Text of Hillary Clinton's Campaign Launch Speech," *Time*, http://time.com/3920332/transcript-full-text-hillary-clinton-campaign-launch/.

Greenlee, J. S., T. Nteta, J. H. Rhodes, and E. Sharrow (2018), "Helping to Break the Glass Ceiling? Fathers, First Daughters, and Presidential Vote Choice in 2016," *Political Behavior*, https://doi.org/10.1007/s11109-018-9514-0.

Sharrow, E., J. H. Rhodes, T. Nteta, and J. S. Greenlee (2018), "The First Daughter Effect: The Impact of Fathering First Daughters on Men's Preferences on Gender Equality Issues," *Public Opinion Quarterly*, 82 (3): 493–523.

Part Five

"Deal Me in": Clinton's Impact on Policy

Preface

Rachel VanSickle-Ward

In recent years, most of the commentary on Clinton has been on her performance as a candidate. This is hardly surprising, given the historic importance of her attempts to break the highest glass ceiling. But it is important to recognize the equally groundbreaking policymaking role she played as a First Lady, Senator and Secretary of State. No presidential candidate before her had her range of policymaking experience. Moreover, her role in policymaking is not confined to policy actions she undertook in office. She also made policy, including the nuts and bolts of policy, a centerpiece in her campaigns. She was so focused on policy on the campaign trail, in fact, that critics contended that she was too wonky, too enamored with policy details.

Clinton's hyper-focus on policy was not something she felt compelled to apologize for, in fact in her DNC acceptance speech she highlighted it as central tenet of her candidacy:

> It's true . . . I sweat the details of policy—whether we're talking about the exact level of lead in the drinking water in Flint, Michigan, the number of mental health facilities in Iowa, or the cost of your prescription drugs. Because it's not just a detail if it's your kid—if it's your family. It's a big deal. And it should be a big deal to your president.

Because she was the first woman to secure the nomination, and because she herself has so often highlighted the significance of women in politics, it's worthwhile to consider how her gender shaped her policymaking accomplishments and agenda. There is a fairly rich literature on gender and policymaking. Numerous studies show that women legislators take distinct policy stances, introduce more bills on "women's issues," employ different rhetoric in floor speeches and bring new perspectives to existing policy discussions (Karpowitz and Mendelberg 2014; Pearson and Dancey 2011a, b; Reingold 2008; Swers 2002, 2013; Mansbridge 1999; VanSickle-Ward and Wallsten 2019). Other work finds more limited or no impact (Barnello 1999; Wolbrecht 2002; Frederick 2009). But because there have been so few women presidential candidates, and no women nominees, we know less about how gender shapes policy in the presidential arena. All the more reason, then, to do a deep dive into the policy platform of the first woman to secure a nomination in a major party—especially one who so frequently emphasized policy in her campaign.

The chapters in Part 5 tackle Clinton's policymaking influence from domestic and international perspectives. They look both at the legacy of specific policies she has formally championed and at how the way in which she framed issues has had broader implications for how we understand policy formation and implementation. Clinton explicitly mainstreamed "women's issues" in both her policy advocacy and her campaign messaging. In so doing, she changed the conversation around whose voices are valued, and who is deserving of a seat at the table in policymaking debates. Because her policy advocacy covers a number of different roles and issues, consideration of Clinton's policy impact helps us better understand her particular legacy, and also tells a broader story of significant policy debates of the past thirty years.

Roselyn Hsueh describes Clinton as a "role model of confident humility, combining expertise and diplomacy" in her approach to foreign policy. Specifically, Hsueh focuses on decisions regarding Benghazi and the Pivot to Asia. She argues that Clinton's foreign policy approach is one of boldness and pragmatism, and that in both success and failure, Clinton emphasized a reliance on known facts over predetermined narratives. Her legacy is seen in the focus on multilateralism in foreign policy and in her willingness to stand her ground, "owning her expertise" despite attempts to delegitimize her.

Sarah Angevine and Celeste Montoya examine Hillary Clinton's impact on American foreign policy with a particular focus on women and girls. Arguing that "no single person has had a greater effect on the representation of women in American foreign policy than Hillary Clinton," Angevine explores three dimensions of this legacy, highlighting key moments and concepts that illustrate each dimension. As First Lady, Clinton raised awareness of the ways that gender is significant in foreign policy decisions, as evidenced by her landmark "women's rights are human rights" address in China. As Secretary of State, she promoted the well-being of women and girls as an important foreign policy outcome, the "Hillary Doctrine." And throughout her career she institutionalized "gender analysis" specifically valuing the voices of women in policy formation, a process that Angevine witnessed first-hand in hearings featuring Afghani women.

Montoya's piece connects the global significance of the "women's rights are human rights" speech to a domestic context. Drawing on the work of intersectional feminists, and her own work on national and transnational efforts to combat violence against women, she argues that "while Clinton's foreign policy approach remained fairly consistent in its tendencies, her approach to domestic women's rights (including violence against women) appeared to be evolving in a more intersectional direction during the course of her campaign."

The focus on the links between Clinton's policy advocacy and broader movements is evident in Ivy Cargile's chapter as well. Cargile argues that "without the ability to vote, democracy ceases to exist." Cargile explores the ways in which Clinton, and the women of color who made up her core supporters, have long focused on voting rights as an essential policy goal. Her piece considers Clinton's long-standing electoral and legislative efforts toward protecting and expanding the franchise, and how she made it a central plank of her 2016 presidential bid. She further explains the critical role women of color have played in the struggle for women's rights, and how the struggle has received renewed attention since 2016.

Rachel VanSickle-Ward and Emma Stephens debunk the oft-repeated myth that Clinton lacked an economic message. Not only did Clinton focus extensively on economic issues on the campaign trail, but, as we explain, she also consciously did so in a way that centerd women: "Deal me in." She highlighted jobs and economic opportunity in discussions of reproductive justice and she proposed bold policies on equal pay and accessible childcare. These issues continue to be pressing, and her policy recommendations continue to be relevant. Her economic message, and how it was heard—or not—offers broader lessons about women's participation in economic policymaking and in their contributions to the economy as a whole.

Finally, Rachel VanSickle-Ward considers Hillary Clinton's legacy as a policy wonk whose approach "powerfully married policy expertise with a validation of women's lived experiences." Drawing on examples from speeches and debate performances, she illustrates that Clinton's willingness to listen and focus on policy details evidenced transparency, boldness, honesty, and seriousness of purpose. This dynamic is particularly noteworthy because, as the first woman to secure a major-party nomination, she elevated women's expertise at a time when that know-how is often sidelined.

References

Barnello, M. A. (1999), "Gender and Roll Call Voting in the New York State Assembly," *Women & Politics*, 20 (4): 77–94.

Frederick, B. (2009), "Are Female House Members Still More Liberal in a Polarized Era? The Conditional Nature of the Relationship Between Descriptive and Substantive Representation," *Congress & the Presidency*, 36 (2): 181–202.

Karpowitz, C. F. and T. Mendelberg (2014), *The Silent Sex: Gender, Deliberation, and Institutions*, Princeton, NJ: Princeton University Press.

Mansbridge, J. (1999), "Should Blacks Represent Blacks and Women Represent Women? A Contingent Yes," *The Journal of Politics*, 61 (3): 628–57.

Pearson, K. and L. Dancey (2011a), "Elevating Women's Voices in Congress: Speech Participation in the House of Representatives," *Political Research Quarterly*, 64 (4): 910–23.

Pearson, K. and L. Dancey (2011b), "Speaking for the Underrepresented in the House of Representatives: Voicing Women's Interests in a Partisan Era," *Politics & Gender*, 7 (4): 493–519.

Reingold, B. (2008), "Women as Office Holders: Linking Descriptive and Substantive Representation," in C. Wolbrecht, K. Beckwith and L. Baldez (eds), *Political Women and American Democracy*, 128–47, New York: Cambridge University Press.

Swers, M. L. (2002), *The Difference Women Make: The Policy Impact of Women in Congress*, 1st ed., Chicago: University of Chicago Press.

Swers, M. L. (2013), *Women in the Club: Gender and Policy Making in the Senate*, Chicago: University of Chicago Press.

VanSickle-Ward, R. and K. Wallsten (2019), *The Politics of the Pill: Gender, Framing and Policymaking in the Battle over Birth Control*, Oxford: Oxford University Press.

Wolbrecht, C. (2002), "Female Legislators and the Women's Rights Agenda: From Feminine Mystique to Feminist Era," *Women Transforming Congress*, Norman: University of Oklahoma Press.

30

Standing Her Ground on Foreign Policy

Roselyn Hsueh

Hillary Clinton became Secretary of State the year I started my current job as a professor of political science. As I searched for my own expert voice and purpose, I saw Clinton as an inspiration. She first prepared for her role as Secretary of State at the Fourth World Conference on Women held in Beijing in 1995. Representing the United States among 180 countries at the conference, the then-First Lady stood her ground, amid pressures to soften her remarks, and declared, "Human rights are women's rights and women's rights are human rights." As a US Senator, Clinton held her own again when she provided leadership as one of the first officials to arrive on the scene in the aftermath of the 9/11 attacks.

This chapter reflects on two policy decisions, which exemplify how, as a stateswoman, Clinton crafted foreign policy based on her values and expertise and justified decisions made under the circumstances and information available to her. First, Clinton's championing of the Obama administration's Pivot to Asia, as part and parcel of the US strategy toward China, showed her commitment to multilateralism and strategic pragmatism. Second, Clinton's cogent responses on the Benghazi attacks, including during subsequent congressional hearings, demonstrated a leadership style grounded in integrity and realism. These two policies are chosen because they are distinct from one another and showcase Clinton's unique brand of multilateralism and her embrace of facts over narratives in responding to twenty-first-century pressures on American power and leadership.

Officially in 2011, and in the diplomatic groundwork laid earlier, Clinton spearheaded then President Obama's foreign policy touchstone, "Pivot to Asia." Clinton touted the "pivot" as an effort to solidify the US relationship with other countries in Asia experiencing pressures born of China's growing assertiveness. This growing assertiveness is rooted in China's globalization strategy. As my first book (Hsueh 2011) shows, China's global economic integration combines economic liberalization with strategic reregulation to achieve state goals oriented around indigenous technological development, global competitiveness of Chinese industry and authoritarian rule.

The US rebalancing toward the Asia Pacific, where half the world's population resides and nearly half of global GDP is found, reasoned that the US global future rests on anticipating and building strong relationships with allies in the region similar to the "post-World War II commitment to building a comprehensive and lasting transatlantic network of institutions and relationships" (Clinton 2011). In the post-Cold War era, to maintain US prosperity and security, economic resources and diplomatic energies for new and renewed relationships would concentrate on working with Asia Pacific allies to forge new markets in lieu of the highly regulated markets in China (which violate China's own commitments to join the World Trade Organization), counter North Korea's nuclear ambitions and defend freedom of navigation in the South China Sea complicated by territorial claims and China's construction of artificial islands.

The architect and public face for this seemingly audacious yet pragmatic stance for the global liberal order, Clinton worked to ensure that the rebalance toward the Asia Pacific focused not just on the US military and diplomatic efforts but also on a multilateral approach (as opposed to China's bilateral dealings). During a trip to Southeast Asia in 2010, Clinton laid out the crux of the US position on maritime disputes in the South China Sea, with China drilling in gas fields in disputed waters and staking claim on nearly all of the islands, reefs and shoals also claimed by Brunei, Malaysia, the Philippines, Taiwan and Vietnam. She emphasized freedom of navigation, respect for international law and US opposition to coercion and support for negotiated settlements (Putz and Tiezzi 2016).

Clinton's diplomatic efforts in the Asia Pacific also paved the way for the Obama administration's Trans-Pacific Partnership (TPP), covering 40 percent of global GDP. The TPP, which did not include China, was designed to expand market and trade opportunities in Asian countries, trade which helped to fuel the US economic recovery after the 2008 financial crisis (Putz and Tiezzi 2016). During her presidential campaign Clinton pulled back on support for the TPP, stating she would "say no to trade deals, like the [TPP,] that do not meet her high standard of raising wages, creating good-paying jobs, and enhancing our national security" (Clinton 2016). This seeming about-turn is in fact consistently Clinton, who first developed her foreign policy credentials in Beijing focused on basic human rights. President Trump, focused on an internally oriented America First platform, officially ended the United States' involvement in the TPP on his first day in office.

In the "pivot to Asia," Clinton pragmatically and boldly led the rebalancing of economic, military, and diplomatic energies in a region both enticed and constrained by China's growing assertiveness. "Clinton had the confidence and stature to stand up to China without going so far as to demonize it" (O'Hanlon 2013). The rebalancing in many regards addressed the three challenges posed by China that my research has identified: Chinese president Xi Jinping is emboldened by China's strategic use of globalization; the new structure of China's economy tests the Asia Pacific region; and China's regional strategy will challenge US leadership (Hsueh 2018).

Unfortunately, Clinton's dashed hopes to become the US president began with the unrelenting partisan Republican-led questioning, in various reports and hearings, of Clinton on the 2012 attacks on the US consulate and CIA outpost in Benghazi, Libya. The attacks on 9/11 that year led to the tragic death of US ambassador Christopher Stevens and three other Americans. What happened in the aftermath of Benghazi was laced with the disdain and double standards often reserved for powerful women with their own vision and purpose, especially if doing so was politically expedient. In contrast, Clinton accepted formal responsibility for the security vulnerabilities while asserting that she did not participate in direct decision-making on consulate security. Importantly, Clinton maintained that an inevitable fog of war after such events led to the administration's varying explanations of what happened immediately following the tragedy. During eleven hours of House Select Committee questioning in October 2015, Clinton sought to focus on "the facts" rather than the political "narrative" of her Republican questioners, which included her use of a private email account and the deliberate or spontaneous origins of the attacks (Gearan, Tumulty, and Viebeck 2015).

The House Select Committee ultimately released competing and partisan final reports, with neither report offering evidence of Clinton's culpability. An earlier report in 2014 of the House Permanent Selection Committee on Intelligence concluded similarly that Obama administration officials did not engage in any wrongdoing. In 2016, Clinton's hometown newspaper did not believe she managed Benghazi "with decisive, principled leadership" (*Chicago Tribune* Op-Ed 2016); however, not unlike like the various congressional investigations, it also did not "find a smoking gun proving that four brave Americans might have been saved."

Political opponents used Benghazi to delegitimize Clinton, but in standing her ground and owning her expertise in the hearing, she demonstrated her trademark resilience and intelligence. The multi-prong legacy of Clinton's Pivot to Asia stands. The foreign policy focused on multilateralism instead of unilateralism, stalwart defense of international law in the face of competing territorial claims and creation of new economic and political opportunities in the context of growing constraints generated by an assertive and authoritarian China bent on maximizing the benefits and minimizing the costs of globalization for the country's own gain (Hsueh 2015). Importantly, Clinton stands as a role model of confident humility, combining expertise and diplomacy.

References

Clinton, H. (2011), "America's Pacific Century," *Foreign Policy* (October 11, 2011).

Clinton, H. (2016), "Labor and Workers' Rights," *Hillary's Vision for America*, The Office of Hillary Rodham Clinton (accessed on January 21, 2019) at https://www.hillaryc linton.com/issues/labor/.

Gearan, A., K. Tumulty, and E. Viebeck (2015), "Clinton, Back in the Benghazi Hot Seat, Withstands Republicans' Grilling," *The Washington Post* (October 22, 2015).

Hsueh, R. (2011), *China's Regulatory State: A New Strategy for Globalization*, Ithaca: Cornell University Press.

Hsueh, R. (2015), "China Manages Capitalism for Its Own Gain. This Explains How," *The Washington Post Monkey Cage* (September 24, 2015).

Hsueh, R. (2018), "China's Three New Economic Challenges for the U.S.," *The Washington Post Monkey Cage* (November 13, 2017).

O'Hanlon, M. E. (2013), "Op-Ed: Missing Clinton's Hand in Asia Rebalance," *Brookings Institution* (December 13, 2013).

"Op-Ed: Benghazi: What the Report Reveals About Hillary Clinton," *Chicago Tribune* (June 28, 2016).

Putz, C. and S. Tiezzi (2016), "Did Clinton Clinton's Pivot to Asia Work?," *The Diplomat* (April 15, 2016).

31

"Women's Rights Are Human Rights"

Celeste Montoya

It is time for us to say here in Beijing, and for the world to hear, that it is no longer acceptable to discuss women's rights as separate from human rights.

If there is one message that echoes forth from this conference, let it be that human rights are women's rights and women's rights are human rights, once and for all.

On 5 September 1995, then First Lady Hillary Rodham Clinton gave a speech at the United Nations' 4th World Conference on Women in Beijing that was later lauded as one of the 100 most significant American political speeches of the twentieth century.[1] A number of factors made this speech so important. First, it helped Clinton establish her individual political identity. The *New York Times* described the speech this way: "Speaking more forcefully on human rights than any American dignitary has on Chinese soil, Hillary Rodham Clinton catalogued a devastating litany of abuse that has afflicted women around the world today and criticized China for seeking to limit free and open discussion of women's issues here."[2] While this individual role was often criticized, it marked an important step in her political trajectory. Clinton's global work on women's human rights likely played an important role in her nomination into Barack Obama's cabinet in 2012 as Secretary of State. She strategically revisited the speech in her 2016 presidential campaign as the first female Democratic Party nominee, commemorating its 20th anniversary in a rally in New Hampshire focused on women's issues.

Beyond what the speech meant to her career, however, was the role it played in framing women's rights as human rights in a global and domestic context. For much of my career as a political scientist, my research has focused on violence against women and movements (national and transnational) aimed at combating it. Framing women's rights as human rights was a pivotal strategy within the transnational movement, one that put the issue of gendered violence on the international agenda and helped push for widespread policy dissemination around the globe (Joachim 1999; Montoya 2013). While Rodham Clinton's framing of women's rights as human rights was a continuation of the strategic work started by a broader network of feminist activists several years earlier (see Bunch 1990), her use of that frame in speaking as the First Lady of the United States on a global stage helped to advance the frame and aid in the momentum of what is often regarded as one of the most successful transnational women's rights movements.

I remember hearing the speech for the first time, and how much it moved me. How inspired I was by those powerful words quoted at the beginning of this chapter. I was not alone. She received a standing ovation. In her memoir *Living History*, she describes her surprise and thrill at how well the message had resonated:

> Delegates rushed to touch me, shout words of appreciation and thank me for coming. Even the delegate from the Vatican commended me for the speech. Outside the hall, women hung over banisters and rushed down escalators to grab my hand. . . . What I didn't know at the time was that my twenty-one minute speech would become a manifesto for women all over the world. To this day, whenever I travel overseas, women come up to me quoting words from the Beijing speech or clutching copies that they want me to autograph.

Clinton's work on global women's rights continued throughout her tenure as First Lady and later as Secretary of State. Her approach to human rights evolved to also encompass and promote LGBT rights. Building on her famous speech, in 2011 she addressed the United Nations on International Human Rights Day: "Like being a woman, like being a racial, religious, tribal, or ethnic minority, being LGBT does not make you less human. And that is why gay rights are human rights, and human rights are gay rights."

It is important to note that Clinton's support for human rights is also a point of contention. Her "hawkish" tendencies as a US Senator and Secretary as State, in particular her stances on the war in Iraq, the Israeli-Palestinian conflict and a coup in Honduras, have been the focus of critique, including by some feminists. During her 2016 campaign, Clinton was also critiqued for her role in supporting the 1994 Crime Bill and the role that it is argued to have played in the mass incarceration of African Americans. Her support was largely in relation to its inclusion of the Violence against Women's Act, widely considered to be one of the most important pieces of legislation addressing gender violence. Feminists of color, however, have long critiqued how anti-violence policy, and universal framings of violence against women more broadly, have had asymmetrical racial and class effects.[3] In particular, women of color who have been victimized are less likely to have access to allocated resources and justice, and men of color are disproportionately prosecuted as perpetrators.

While Clinton's foreign policy approach remained fairly consistent in its tendencies, her approach to domestic women's rights (including violence against women) appeared to be evolving in a more intersectional direction during the course of her campaign. In numerous speeches she used the term or the language of intersectionality in addressing the ways in which gender, race, class (and other forms of structural inequality) work together. For example, in a speech in Harlem, she stated, "We face a complex set of economic, social, and political challenges. They are intersectional, they are reinforcing, and we have got to take them all on." In a speech at a Planned Parenthood Action Fund event, she discussed reproductive rights as inextricable from other issues, such as the minimum wage, equal pay, passing comprehensive immigration reform and challenging systemic racism, "All the issues we're talking about today are connected. They intersect. . . . All those issues go straight to that fundamental question: whether we believe women and families of all races and backgrounds and income levels deserve an equal shot in life."

This use of intersectionality is important. The feminist mobilizing that has risen in the wake of her defeat and the election of Donald Trump has taken a more intersectional turn. This is largely the work of feminists at the intersection of multiple oppression, but it is not insignificant that Clinton helped introduce the term and the ideas to new audiences. Whether her use of intersectionality was a campaign strategy or an authentic change in perspective, once again, she used her position in the public spotlight to advance a frame of women's rights that may become transformational.

References

Bunch, C. (1990), "Toward a Re-vision of Human Rights," *Human Rights Quarterly,* 12: 486–98.

Clinton, H. R. (2004), *Living History*, New York: Scribner.

Crenshaw, K. (1991), "Mapping the Margins: Intersectionality, Identity Politics, and Violence Against Women of Color," *Stanford Law Review*, 43 (6): 1241–99.

Davis, A. (1983), *Women, Race & Class*, New York: Vintage Books.

Joachim, J. (1999), "Shaping the Human Rights Agenda: The Case of Violence Against Women," in M. K. Meyer and E. Prügl (eds), *Gender Politics in Global Governance*, 142–60, Lanham, MD: Rowman & Littlefield.

Montoya, C. (2013), *From Global to Grassroots: The European Union, Transnational Advocacy, and Combating Violence Against Women*, New York: Oxford University Press.

Richie, B. (1996), *Compelled to Crime: The Gender Entrapment of Battered Black Women*, New York: Routledge.

Richie, B. (2000), "A Black Feminist Reflection on the Antiviolence Movement," *Signs: Journal of Women in Culture and Society*, 25 (4): 1133–7.

Tyler, P. (1995), "Hillary Clinton, in China, Details Abuse of Women," *The New York Times* (September 6, 1995).

Global Gender Effects

The Impact of Hillary Clinton on American Foreign Policy

Sara Angevine

As a US First Lady, as a US Senator, as a US Secretary of State and as a US presidential candidate, Hillary Clinton has consistently drawn attention to the importance of women and girls worldwide, expanding the parameters of historically male-dominated American foreign policy. Clinton's most significant effect on American foreign policy is that she directed attention toward the importance of gender globally. In my research on the representation of women in American foreign policy, I find that prioritizing women and girls is rarely a policy consideration (Angevine 2014). Hillary Clinton changed that. Thus, I suggest that no single person has had a greater effect on the representation of women in American foreign policy than Hillary Clinton.

The three lasting ways Clinton changed the trajectory of American foreign policy are by (1) educating the US electorate and global populations that gender *matters* to foreign policy; (2) prioritizing the advancement of the status of women and girls worldwide as an American foreign policy *outcome*, that is, the Hillary Doctrine (Hudson and Leidl 2015)[1]; and (3) institutionalizing gender analysis and including the voices of women in the American foreign policy construction *process*. By expanding American foreign policy public opinion, priorities and processes to include the role of gender, Clinton arguably improved the lives of women worldwide.

First, building on her famous "women's rights are human rights" speech in Beijing, China (as discussed by Montoya, this volume), First Lady Hillary Clinton (1992–2000) directed American foreign policy conversations to address issues facing women. In her public speeches, Clinton would argue how gender matters to American foreign policy. On her 2016 presidential campaign website,

Clinton even claimed that she would "promote women's rights around the globe" as one of her top priorities.[2] Though Hillary Clinton was not elected as US president, by drawing attention to the importance of women's human rights on the campaign trail, she deepened the gender awareness of the US electorate and shaped American foreign policy public opinion. This frame of global women's rights may have created a new space for women candidates to show American foreign policy competence, an area where studies show that they are often ranked lower than men candidates (Lawless 2004; Dolan 2010; see also Holman, Merolla, and Zechmeister in this volume).

Second, Hillary Clinton placed the advancement of the status of women and girls as an important American foreign policy outcome, known as the Hillary Doctrine (Hudson and Leidl 2016). The seeds of this began when Hillary Clinton was First Lady, when she promoted the appointment of the first female US Secretary of State (Madeline Albright), ensured that more USAID dollars were directed toward funding women's needs than ever before and co-founded the global women's rights organization, Vital Voices: Women in Democracy (Garner 2013). Clinton has long argued that the participation of women, the security of women, and the leadership of women is vital to global security, economic development and the overall health of communities. After Hillary Clinton (D-NY) was elected as US Senator (2001–2008), she took her global women's rights foreign policy agenda to Congress, sponsoring three and cosponsoring ten other bills that focused on advancing the status of women and girls in foreign countries. Of these thirteen women's foreign policy bills, the Afghan Women and Children Relief Act of 2001 was ultimately signed into law (a rarity in terms of women's foreign policy legislation).

Next, as US Secretary of State from 2009–2013, Clinton established over forty-five new programs that focused on advancing the status of women and girls in foreign countries. The Iraqi Women's Democracy Initiative, the Global Women, Peace and Security Initiative, Global Alliance for Clean Cookstoves, Pacific Women's Empowerment Initiative, Empowering Women and Girls Through Sports Initiative and the Child Marriage Initiative are just a few of the numerous programs Clinton was able to put into place during her tenure as US Secretary of State. In addition, President Obama's creation of the US National Action Plan on Women, Peace and Security, the Ambassador-At-Large for Global Women's Issues and the Office of Global Women's Issues in the Department of State are primarily the result of Clinton's leadership. Secretary Clinton required that the interpretation and implementation of all American foreign policy include a gender analysis. Gender training programs became expected rather than optional. Doing a gender analysis of the impact of any program became routine rather than rare.

Finally, Hillary Clinton had an effect on the gender dynamics inside the American foreign policy construction process, a pattern I observed first-hand when she was US Senator (D-NY). Prior to 9/11, the Taliban was known to many in the US feminist community for their harsh treatment of women and girls. Soon after the 9/11 attacks, President George W. Bush and First Lady Laura Bush drew attention to the Taliban's treatment of women and focused on the importance of liberating these oppressed women. Scholars contend that this "save the women" trope galvanized domestic support for US military intervention, while delegitimizing Afghani women's agency in the process (Sheperd 2006; Ferguson 2005; Young 2003).

This was a unique time for American feminism, American foreign policy, and global human rights. The American feminist community was divided (Hunt 2006), concerned about the harm women faced under the Taliban as well as the harm women could face under US military intervention. The US-based Feminist Majority Foundation (FMF) was center stage in this debate, and as an undergraduate intern with FMF at the time (Fall 2001), I happened to be in the first few rows to observe. Inside of this tumultuous context, I witnessed Senator Hillary Clinton expand the American foreign policymaking process to include the voices of women, reflecting democratic and feminist principles of equality and inclusion in decision-making.

On November 29, 2001, Senator Clinton partnered with the FMF to bring Afghani women to testify to the US Congress in a hearing titled "Future of Afghan Women." Four exiled Afghani women spoke while many other Afghani women sat in the audience, alongside myself and the other American FMF interns. Although these women had no authority over the construction of American foreign policy in the US political system, they were able to voice their interests, and nine US Senators attended the hearing to listen. Upon reviewing the transcript of this hearing, now through my lens as a gender politics scholar, one moment stood out to me as encapsulating Clinton's approach to redefining the American foreign policy construction process. She closed with the following questions to her panel:

> When someone like me or my colleagues Senator Mikulski or Senator Cantwell speak out about the rights of women in Afghanistan and we are told that we are trying to impose our views, our beliefs, our ideas of rights on your society. . . . Can you help me to give the best answer that I can give to anyone that says "You as an American woman have no right to ask for rights for Afghan women

and the American government has no right to tell the Afghani people they must have women at the table to be a part of a government"? Will you help us with the best answer to the question, which we are often asked? (Senator Hillary Clinton, November 29, 2001)

Clinton is basically asking these Afghani women how, as a US Senator advocating for Afghani women's rights, she can best serve as an ally. Her questions also reflect the complexity of the United States (or any country) advocating for the advancement of women's rights in a foreign country.

In sum, Hillary Rodham Clinton expanded and transformed American foreign policy public opinion, outcomes and processes to include and understand the importance of women and girls. Her lasting global gender effect on American foreign policy continues to be felt, both in the United States and worldwide. Though studies show that advancing the status of women expands economies (Duflo 2012), improves the health of communities (Garrett 2007), strengthens democracy (Inglehart and Norris 2003), advances education (Coleman 2004) and reduces terrorism (Hudson et al. 2012), it requires the political will to prioritize advancing the status of women as a foreign policy objective. Hillary Clinton has that will and the world is better off because of it.

References

Angevine, S. (2014), *Women's Rights Foreign Policy in the US Congress: Policy Objectives, Congressional Motivations, and the Role of Policy Entrepreneurs* (Doctoral dissertation, Rutgers University-Graduate School, New Brunswick).

Bunch, C. (1990), "Women's Rights as Human Rights: Toward a Re-vision of Human Rights," *Human Rights Quarterly*, 12: 486–98.

Coleman, I. (2004), "The Payoff from Women's Rights," *Foreign Affairs*, 83: 80.

Dolan, K. (2010), "The Impact of Gender Stereotyped Evaluations on Support for Women Candidates," *Political Behavior*, 32 (1): 69–88.

Duflo, E. (2012), "Women Empowerment and Economic Development," *Journal of Economic Literature*, 50 (4): 1051–79.

Ferguson, M. L. (2005), "'W' Stands for Women: Feminism and Security Rhetoric in the Post-9/11 Bush Administration," *Politics & Gender*, 1 (1): 9–38.

Future of Afghani Women: General Hearing, Senate, 107th Cong. 1 (2001).

Garner, K. (2013), *Gender and Foreign Policy in the Clinton Administration*, Boulder, CO: FirstForumPress.

Garrett, L. (2007), "The Challenge of Global Health," *Foreign Affairs*, 1: 14–38.

Hook, S. W. and J. Spanier (2018), *American Foreign Policy Since World War II*, Washington, DC: CQ Press.

Hudson, V. M. and P. Leidl (2015), *The Hillary Doctrine: Sex and American Foreign Policy*, New York City: Columbia University Press.

Hudson, V. M., M. Caprioli, C. F. Emmett, and B. Ballif-Spanvill (2012), *Sex and World Peace*, New York City: Columbia University Press.

Hunt, K. (2006), "'Embedded Feminism' and the War on Terror," in Krista Hunt and Kim Rygiel (eds), *Gendering the War on Terror: War Stories and Camouflaged Politics*, 51–71, Abingdon, UK: Routledge Press.

Hurlburt, H. (2016), "Was Hillary Clinton a Good Secretary of State?," *CNN.com*, July 29, https://www.cnn.com/2016/07/28/opinions/clinton-secretary-of-state-opinion-hurlburt/index.html (accessed November 20, 2018).

Inglehart, R. and P. Norris (2003), *Rising Tide: Gender Equality and Cultural Change Around the World*, Cambridge: Cambridge University Press.

Keck, M. E. and K. Sikkink (2014), *Activists Beyond Borders: Advocacy Networks in International Politics*, New York: Cornell University Press.

Lawless, J. L. (2004), "Women, War, and Winning Elections: Gender Stereotyping in the Post-September 11th Era," *Political Research Quarterly*, 57 (3): 479–90.

Merry, S. E. (2009), *Human Rights and Gender Violence: Translating International Law into Local Justice*, Chicago: University of Chicago Press.

Shepherd, L. J. (2006), "Veiled References: Constructions of Gender in the Bush Administration Discourse on the Attacks on Afghanistan Post-9/11," *International Feminist Journal of Politics*, 8 (1): 19–41.

Young, I. M. (2003), "The Logic of Masculinist Protection: Reflections on the Current Security State," *Signs: Journal of Women in Culture and Society*, 29 (1): 1–25.

The Backbone of Democracy

Clinton, Women of Color and the Fight for Voting Rights

Ivy A. M. Cargile

The 116th Congress has a House of Representatives that is not just diverse but also has the most women elected to the chamber in US history. As this milestone is being celebrated, it is also the case that the United States continues to grapple with attempts by several states at restricting the vote. During the 2018 midterm elections states such as Georgia and North Carolina are alleged to have purged 10 percent of names from their voter rolls, while Florida is said to have removed 7 percent.[1] Without the ability to vote, democracy ceases to exist. It is a vehicle for people to have a voice and in so doing, elect those who they think are the best suited to represent them and their interests.

Hillary Clinton has long known this. In 2013, she began to issue serious warnings about this type of attack on democracy. Before she decided to run for the presidency in 2016, she was arguing that what the attack on the ballot box represented was a "sweeping effort to dis-empower and disenfranchise people of color, poor people, and young people" (Roth, 2015). However, her fight for voting rights did not start then. In the early 1970s she registered Latino voters as a volunteer for the George McGovern campaign. As a Senator in 2005, Clinton attempted to secure and expand the franchise by proposing the Count Every Vote Act,[2] which among other things sought to make Election Day a holiday, and to re-enfranchise ex-felons who had paid their debt to society. While she was unsuccessful in getting this bill passed, it proves her commitment to maintaining a vibrant democracy even before she decided to run for the presidency.

As a part of her vision for voting rights Clinton sought to expand the right to vote, not limit it. In a speech she gave during her presidential bid at Texas

Southern University,[3] the alma mater of Barbara Jordan, one of the most ardent fighters for the Voting Rights Act of 1965, Clinton bemoaned the 2013 Supreme Court decision in *Shelby County v Holder* (2013)[4] that guts a key section of the law. In the majority decision, states with a history of discrimination when it comes to voting no longer have to seek federal approval to change their voting laws. This section of the Voting Rights Act, known as the *pre-clearance* section,[5] was meant to ensure that states were not arbitrarily placing obstacles to voting that all citizens are guaranteed under the US Constitution. Furthermore, what this ruling did is allow for the application of harmful laws such as the voter id laws put forth by various states in the name of voter fraud. What has resulted is that these laws have in fact depressed voter turnout (Ansolabehere and Hersh 2017), particularly the turnout of voters of color, low-income individuals, and young voters—specifically college students. As Clinton noted in her 2013 speech, this is not where the longest lasting democracy in history should be. Instead, it should be making the franchise more accessible so that citizens can have their voices heard.

In thinking about voting as the mechanism for representation, it is understandable why Clinton's loss was devastating to many. However, in the aftermath we can see that in the sense of loss, inspiration, and resilience bloomed. The Women's Marches that were quickly organized and took place stemmed from women seeking to continue the fight against the sexism and racism that the new president represented. During the second Women's March in 2018, participants were reminded not just to march but to vote through the organization of "power to the polls,"[6] which was the march's national voter registration, education, and mobilization campaign. For African American women, the marches were a way to represent their own interests and those of individuals who could not be there due to safety concerns (Bunyasi and Smith 2018). After showing up to the polls on Election Day 2016, women of color felt a sense of urgency to make it known that what the incoming administration represented was going to be resisted and challenged at every turn. Women of color who represented a large percentage of Clinton's electoral base,[7] particularly African American women, are keenly aware that one of the most effective ways of ensuring policy change is through electoral politics (Tate 1998). This is why we see Clinton's core supporters—African American, Asian American, and Latina women—participate electorally to try and ensure that rights already won through previous movements would not be lost. For these three groups of women, who represent an intersection of race/ethnicity and gender, Clinton represented the protection of civil rights, the Affordable Care Act and their reproductive rights, but most importantly, the protection of the ballot box. Specifically, because in the end it is this last protection—that of ensuring the vote[8]—that will safeguard the others.

Her commitment to voting rights is one of the many reasons that Clinton's loss was shattering. However, in facing the challenge of the loss, historic numbers of women chose to harness their power not just by voting but also by running for political office in 2018. In the years following the 2016 election, the power of women of color at the ballot box, particularly of African American women (see Virginia and Alabama 2017 election results), became evident. This translated not just into more women of color voting but also running for office, which is why we see so many women of color running for all levels of office and, consequently, making history by winning seats[9] that had never before had a woman or a woman of color elected to them.

All the women who ran, whether they lost or won, are examples of why Hillary Clinton is so pivotal to American politics. Of course, she matters because she was so close to busting through that ultimate glass ceiling but more importantly it is because of her beliefs and policy positions. Voters believe in her because issues like voting rights are vital to her. This matters to her not because voter suppression may have caused her to lose key votes but because she has been fighting for this issue for decades. Voting rights are the backbone of democracy. Not only do they allow for citizens' voices to be heard but they also allow for the government to be a representative body—a government for the people by the people. Clinton, and the communities of color who supported her, have long understood this. Given that the first bill introduced by the 116th Congress seeks to expand voting rights, it is clear that the women who have followed in her footsteps understand this as well.

References

Ansolabehere, S. and E. D. Hersh (2017), "ADGN: An Algorithm for Record Linkage Using Address, Date of Birth, Gender, and Name," *Statistics and Public Policy*, 4 (1): 1–10.

Bunyasi, T. L. and C. W. Smith (2018), "Get in Formation: Black Women's Participation in the Women's March on Washington as an Act of Pragmatic Utopianism," *The Black Scholar*, 48 (3): 4–16.

'Exit Polls 2014,' https://www.cnn.com/election/2016/results/exit-polls (accessed January 5, 2019).

Roth, Z. (2013), "Hillary Clinton lays out sweeping voting rights vision," http://www.msnbc.com/msnbc/hillary-clinton-early-voting-nationwide (accessed February 15, 2019).

Tate, K. (1998), *From Protest to Politics: The New Black Voters in American Elections*, New York: Russell Sage Foundation.

The "Economic Woman"

Why Clinton's Economic Message Still Matters

Rachel VanSickle-Ward and Emma Stephens

Of all the narratives critiquing Clinton's 2016 presidential run, perhaps the most persistent is the argument that her campaign neglected economic issues, supposedly alienating "working-class" voters.[1] Careful observers have pushed back on this narrative, noting that she in fact spoke extensively on economic issues and proposed a range of policies to address them.[2] In fact, she referenced jobs, the economy and workers more than anything else in her public addresses during the 2016 campaign.[3] Moreover, poorer voters[4] were more likely to vote for her, and voters most concerned with the economy favored her.[5] Scholars have shown that attitudes on race was a more significant factor in predicting support for Trump than economic dissatisfaction (Schaffner, MacWilliams, and Nteta 2018; Reny, Collingwood, and Valenzuela 2019). Looking specifically at voters who switched from Obama in 2012 to Trump 2016, for example, Reny, Collingwood, and Valenzuela note that "white voters with racially conservative or anti-immigrant attitudes switched votes to Trump at a higher rate than those with more liberal views on these issues," (109) and that "vote switching was more associated with racial and immigration attitudes than economic factors" (91).

So why does this myth persist? The problem could lie in how her campaign was covered—her policy proposals, including economic proposals, received very little coverage,[6] and she received less coverage overall than Trump (Patterson 2016). More broadly, they illustrate a number of problems with how we talk about women and the economy—or whether we talk about them at all.

Not only did Clinton consistently talk about economic issues, but she also frequently and explicitly did so in a way that centerd women. She incorporated discussion of jobs and economic opportunity into speeches about reproductive justice.[7] She spoke often about the significance of equal pay[8] and accessible childcare.[9] Rather than sidelining "women's issues" as minor, she argued that fair economic policies for women were essential not just for women themselves but also for the families they often supported, and for the economy as a whole.[10] Indeed, a central tenet of her campaign was that "women's issues" *are* "economic issues." One of her most repeated phrases on the stump highlighted the link between women's rights and economic policy: "If fighting for women's health care and paid family leave and equal pay is playing the woman card, then *deal me in.*"

This approach was not accidental. As political scientist Kelly Dittmar noted, "Her message was consistent with an idea featured formally at the [United Nations' Fourth World Conference on Women in Beijing] to move gender equality to the forefront of policy and political agendas: what the UN has titled 'gender mainstreaming.'"[11]

Clinton has been centring women's rights for decades.[12] There may have been strategic benefits to continuing this approach during her 2016 presidential campaign. Historically (Wolbrecht et al. 2008), women candidates have been more likely to be trusted on issues that deal with caretaking and compassion such as health care, education, and welfare. In contrast, men are, on balance, more likely to be trusted on economic, public safety, and national security policy. Clinton and her campaign advisers may have believed she would have more credibility on economic issues if she "played to her strengths" by framing these issues with a gender equality and caretaking focus. Whatever the motivation in 2016, Clinton has since continued to emphasize the links between gender inequality and economic inequality.[13] And, it is worth noting, she continues to warn about the fundamental dangers of economic inequality in general, arguing that "massive economic inequality and corporate monopoly power are antidemocratic and corrode the American way of life."[14]

The framing of economic issues often minimizes and curtails discussion of gender. This has been attributed by scholars to a host of factors (Nelson and Ferber 2003). Unpaid work in the economy, for child and elder care for example, is often done by women, but does not show up in national economic statistics. Women are underrepresented within the economics discipline itself, and neoclassical economic assumptions about a universal "economic man" within many economic models have constrained analyses of human interactions and interrelationships in a way that tends to omit the lived experiences of many, particularly women. These facts may serve as an additional explanation for the narrative that Clinton did not have an economic message: the language traditionally used in economics that keeps gender on the sidelines may have additionally impacted the ability of some observers to recognize Clinton's economic messages, given their explicit inclusion of gender. This is despite the fact that her economic plans were widely endorsed by economists themselves.[15]

Feminist economists would argue that gender mainstreaming economic policy in this way not only benefits women by highlighting unequal economic outcomes across genders but also provides valuable insights on economic processes at work for everyone. But the lack of resonance with previous economic policy speeches that do not typically use this language might have added to the perception that the message was missing.

This is not to say that there aren't valid critiques of Clinton's economic plans or message. Nor do we suggest that her framing was without risk. Indeed, there is evidence that elevating women is perceived by some men as a threat to their status. Political scientist Dan Cassino sums it up this way: "Men used to run everything. And now they don't, and Hillary Clinton is the apotheosis of these fears."[16]

But her message, and how we evaluate it, is significant far beyond perceptions of one candidacy. Indeed, as other chapters in this volume show, a number of women who ran in 2018 highlighted their gender in frank and groundbreaking ways. Some of these tie directly to tangible economic issues, such as how to pay for childcare while on the campaign[17] trail or when serving in Congress[18]. Illyse Hogue, president of NARAL pro-choice America, sees promise in 2018 state election results for policies that benefit women's economic outlook, stating that "the pro-choice victories we saw in the House, in governors mansions, and in state legislatures across the country were critical steps in building the infrastructure for passing policies that help women achieve greater economic stability in this country."[19]

More broadly, inclusion of women's experiences into economic policy discussions makes for better economic policy and signals that women's voices are worth hearing. Invalidating or erasing those messages implies that "women's economic issues" are not "real economic issues." And it reinforces the notion that women are less worthy of a seat at the table where economic decisions are made. Women's health care, paid family leave and equal pay remain pressing economic issues that are too often omitted or downplayed in economic policy narratives. More careful attention to policies that lead to tangible economic improvements for everyone will be needed on the road ahead. Clinton's "deal me in" approach to gender mainstreaming in economic policy remains as vital as ever.

References

Nelson, M. A. and J. A. Ferber (2003), *Feminist Economics Today: Beyond Economic Man*, Chicago: University of Chicago Press.

Patterson, T. E. (2016), "News Coverage of the 2016 General Election: How the Press Failed the Voters," https://shorensteincenter.org/news-coverage-2016-general-election/.

Reny, T. T., L. Collingwood, and A. Valenzuela (2019), "Vote Switching in the 2016 Election: How Racial and Immigration Attitudes, Not Economics, Explain Shifts in White Voting," *Public Opinion Quarterly*, 83 (1): 91–113.

Schaffner, B. F., M. MacWilliams, and T. Nteta (2018), "Understanding White Polarization in the 2016 Vote for President: The Sobering Role of Racism and Sexism," *Political Science Quarterly*, 133 (1): 9–34.

Wolbrecht, C., K. Beckwith, and L. Baldez (2008), *Political Women and American Democracy*, New York: Cambridge University Press.

The Wisdom of a Wonky Woman

Reflecting on Clinton's Approach to Policy on the Campaign Trail

Rachel VanSickle-Ward

Hillary Clinton was masterful on the debate stage. One political commentator declared her forays as "the most effective series of debate performances in modern political history."[1] The public response was favorable on balance as well.[2] Of particular note, Clinton's third and final debate performance in the general election powerfully married policy expertise with a validation of women's lived experiences. Her answers illustrated in-depth knowledge on a range of issues, reinforcing her reputation as a prepared policy wonk. But she also highlighted women's personal experiences as relevant and authoritative. In a rebuttal to Trump on abortion she argued, with clear passion, "You should meet with some of the woman I've met with, women I've known." Regarding Trump's treatment of women, she stated: "Donald thinks belittling women makes him bigger, he goes after their dignity, their self-worth, I don't think there is a woman anywhere who doesn't know what that feels like." Citing "everyday" examples to illustrate broader themes is hardly new in political debates; in fact, it is quite a common device. But watching the first woman to participate as a candidate in a general election presidential debate argue forcefully that women's voices matter in the policies that affect us was remarkable indeed.[3]

Clinton's emphasis on women's knowledge throughout her campaign is particularly significant because recognition of that knowledge is too often lacking in political discourse. In my book with Kevin Wallsten on birth control policy, for example, we document that "regulating reproduction is rooted in struggles over equality, [and over] whose expertise is deemed worthy, and whose voice is amplified" (VanSickle-Ward and Wallsten 2019). All too frequently, on issues that affect women in concrete, sometimes life and death, ways our voices are excluded from public narratives, and our expertise diminished and devalued. From watching Anita Hill testify about her experience with sexual harassment before an all-male Senate Judiciary committee during the Clarence Thomas confirmation hearings, to an all-male panel opposing expanded access to birth control under the Affordable Care Act, the image of deliberation over women's health or well-being with no women at the table is, sadly, an all-too-familiar sight.

In contrast, Clinton's approach to health care policy specifically and policy more generally has long been grounded in women's expertise—her own, born of decades of experience fighting for universal health care, and those she listens to and learns from. Take, for example, her first speech after becoming the presumptive Democratic nominee given to Planned Parenthood Action Fund. In the address,[4] she extensively credited activists and health care providers for their work, noted her legal expertise on the topic, and called for specific policy action such as repealing the Hyde Amendment.[5] Moreover she argued, as she did throughout her campaign that "women's issues" ought to be front and center:

> For too long, issues like [reproductive rights] have been dismissed by many as "women's issues"—as though that somehow makes them less worthy, secondary. Well, yes, these are women's issues. They're also family issues. They're economic issues. They're justice issues. They're fundamental to our country and our future.

The fact that Clinton took a place at the table that women never had before matters a great deal, but it is equally as important that in claiming that place, she explicitly insisted that women deserved to be there. She spoke as a woman who knew what she was talking about, knew that lots of other women do as well and was intent on translating that knowledge into workable policy.

Other chapters in the volume (Feeley, Angevine) have discussed how often and effectively Clinton listens in both campaigning and policymaking. In a profile of her for Vox, Ezra Klein commented on this dynamic as well:[6]

> Clinton, in her travels, stuffed notes from her conversations and her reading into suitcases, and every few months she dumped the stray paper on the floor of her Senate office and picked through it with her staff. The card tables were for categorization: scraps of paper related to the environment went here, crumpled clippings related to military families there. These notes, [aide] Rubiner recalls, really did lead to legislation. Clinton took seriously the things she was told, the things she read, the things she saw. She made her team follow up.

The flipside of listening is the ability to communicate what you've heard, and how you're going to respond. Clinton famously communicated her fundamental "stronger together" message through policy proposals. She offered detailed policy reform on pressing, thorny issues like health care, gun violence, racial inequality and economic inequality. Offering some policy agenda is more or less expected of a modern presidential candidate, but the depth and detail with which she talked about policy on the campaign trail was unique. There has been no shortage of critics of this approach—policy, we are frequently told, is not as compelling as "vision"—but offering concrete policy illustrates tremendous courage, transparency, and honesty. Ironically, of course, these are the very qualities Clinton supposedly lacked.

For all the false narratives about Clinton's supposed dishonestly, she is fundamentally honest about governing. She speaks not just about the challenges we face but also about how to best solve them. In delving into detail in her policy proposals, she took a considerable risk—vague promises or platitudes are easier because there is less to oppose or take issue with. In my book on policy construction, *The Devil is in the Details* (2014), I argue that ambiguity serves as a vehicle for compromise when key participants disagree over details. Specific policy is often trickier, particularly on high-profile issues in a polarized political context; it engenders more opposition and is harder to pass. Committing herself to concrete policy was not a prosaic choice, it was actually remarkable bold. In so doing, Clinton opened herself up to attack over the details; details she could have glossed over in hopes that conflicting groups would assume she meant whatever they wanted her to mean. The benefits of her approach were transparency and accountability. Ambiguous policy statements sometimes kick conflict down the road, while specific proposals enter into that conflict head on, and allow those affected by policies to respond to specific claims and to track whether policies were in fact delivered.

More broadly, political campaigns that focus on policy signal a basic recognition that laws affect people's lives. As she noted in her speech accepting the Democratic nomination (referenced in the preface): "It's not just a detail if it's your kid—if it's your family. It's a big deal. And it should be a big deal to your president." The seriousness with which Clinton addressed policy, and the extent to which she listened to those most affected by it, serves as a guidepost in a culture where too often politics is treated merely as a game.

The legacy of the policy-centerd approach is evident in the 2020 presidential campaign. Perhaps the clearest example is the candidacy of Elizabeth Warren, whose wonkiness is so central to her image that "Warren has a plan for that" t-shirts are available on her campaign website. Clinton's elevation of "women's issues" into the national conversation has had a lasting impact as well. Warren has spoken extensively on the need for Universal Child Care; Senator Kamala Harris has championed policies to tackle the gender pay gap, and focused on the particular challenges faced by black women. On abortion policy, pay equity, childcare, paid family leave, and so many other topics, Democratic candidates are continuing the call to "deal me in," and even upping the ante.[7]

On 26 July 2016, the night that Hillary Clinton became the first woman ever nominated for president by a major party, my young daughter excitedly said, "The best part was when she thanked the girls who stayed up late, she was talking to me!" In the moment, I was too moved to speak. Reflecting now on how often throughout her career she has spoken to, and about, girls and women, how often she has listened to us and how often those conversations made their way into the details of policies she promoted, I can confidently say, "Yes, she is talking to me, too."

References

VanSickle-Ward, R. (2014), *The Devil Is in the Details: Understanding the Causes of Policy Specificity and Ambiguity*, New York: SUNY Press.

VanSickle-Ward, R. and K. Wallsten (2019), *The Politics of the Pill: Gender Framing and Policymaking in the Battle over Birth Control*, New York: Oxford University Press.

Conclusion

Jennifer L. Merolla and Rachel VanSickle-Ward

On January 3, 2019, Hillary Clinton tweeted a congratulatory message to the women of the 116th Congress: "To the women sworn into Congress today, the most in our history: Congratulations. Knock it out of the park."[1] Ilhan Omar, one of the newly elected members featured in the pictures highlighted by Clinton, responded: "Thank you for the love, @HillaryClinton. Women like you have paved the way for all of us to have come this far."[2]

As this volume has shown, one of the lasting legacies of Hillary Clinton has been as a role model, paving the way for more women to step into the electoral arena. For the first time in US history, over 100 women are in the US House. Thirty-two of these women were newly elected in 2018. Certainly, some women were inspired to run as a reaction against Donald Trump, but there was also an independent effect in seeing Clinton run for the highest office of the land. Women like Denise Davis, who shared her story of Clinton's impact, became inspired to throw her hat into the ring, and this effect was found more broadly in research recounted by Kanthak in this volume.

Even for those who may not have been as directly inspired by Clinton, her election as the Democratic nominee, and visibility during the general election, sent a signal that women belong in politics. Her runs for office have shown how women can bring their varied strengths to the table, from listening tours (as discussed by Feeley) to their roles as daughters, mothers and grandmothers (as noted by VanSickle-Ward and Greenlee), to emphasizing their policy and governing expertise, to reaching out to diverse groups to build community (as discussed by Pantoja and Bejarano). She has shown how women can counter stereotypes of women being weak on national security on the campaign trail (as noted by Holman, Merolla, and Zechmeister). And she is a source of strength to activists and advocates, connecting them to struggles past and present (as discussed by Osborn and Dominguez).

As a testament to this shift in perceptions of belonging, a record number of women ran for the Democratic nomination for president in 2020 than ever before. Elizabeth Warren (Senator of Massachusetts) and Kamala Harris (Senator of California) declared their candidacy early, in January of 2019. Soon after their announcements, Amy Klobuchar (Senator or Minnesota), Tulsi Gabbard (Representative of Hawaii), and Kirstin Gillibrand (Senator of New York) joined the fray.[3] While Joe Biden won the Democratic nomination, the sheer number of women who ran just one election after Clinton's run is nothing short of remarkable.

After a tough election loss, Clinton did not fade away into the shadows. She has refused to stay silent and "learn to knit"[4] just as she refused, all those years ago, to host teas and bake cookies. Rather, she started a nonprofit, Onward Together, which seeks to provide support for organizations that are advancing progressive values. It partners with organizations to encourage more individuals to become active and run for office. Some of its earliest partners included Color of Change, Emerge America, Indivisible, Swing Left, and Run for Something. Many of these groups were important in encouraging more women, people of color and young people to run for office, and many played an instrumental role in flipping the House blue in 2018. A recent partner, the National Domestic Workers Alliance, supports policy advocacy on labor and immigrant rights.

This legacy of women running for and winning high-profile public office, and her own continued work in the public sphere is striking, but the conclusions of our work illustrate that Clinton's legacy persists in ways that may not always make headlines. She has helped shape political activism among women, across generational divides. She has changed the way young children imagine the political space (see, for example, the contributions by Wood; Greenlee, Bos, Holman, Lay, and Oxley), and who makes up that space. Her legacy has also resulted in more subtle shifts in how we view women in power in a variety of settings, and in how women view their own potential (see Sarathy and Cohen in this volume). She has shown that we are not imposters, but transformational leaders, mentors, scholars, and advocates, who will not be silent or silenced.

Notes

Introduction

1 https://www.nytimes.com/2016/07/29/us/politics/hillary-clinton-dnc-transcript. html.
2 https://www.ohchr.org/Documents/Issues/Women/ViolenceAgainstWomeninPol iticsReport.pdf.
3 https://www.rollingstone.com/politics/politics-features/meet-the-women-inspired-to-run-for-office-after-the-2016-election-112336/.
4 https://www.washingtonpost.com/news/monkey-cage/wp/2016/11/14/even-in-defeat-clintons-campaign-could-still-inspire-young-women/?noredirect=on& utm_term=.65b579b1746d

Preface

1 https://faculty.wagner.edu/lori-weintrob/hilary-clinton-an-empowering-woman-of-the-21st-century/
2 Here we focus on Clinton as a role model for adults beyond running for office. In other sections, we discuss the literature on role model effects for children, and focus more specifically on the impact of role models in leading women to run for office and shaping their campaigns.
3 At the same time, other scholars find that these effects are more mixed and limited; especially once partisanship is taken into account (Lawless 2004; Dolan 2006; Reingold and Harrell 2010).

Chapter 1

1 See the ranking of women in national parliaments by the Inter-Parliamentary Union: http://archive.ipu.org/wmn-e/classif.htm.
2 Zhou (2016) and Friedman (2017).
3 Full text available at https://www.wellesley.edu/events/commencement/archives/ 2017/commencementaddress.

Chapter 2

1 https://www.washingtonpost.com/wp-srv/politics/special/clinton/stories/flowers01
   2792.htm.
2 https://www.nytimes.com/2016/11/06/us/politics/hillary-clinton-cookies.html.

Chapter 3

1 On Clinton's 2000 Senate race, see also Anderson (2002), Scharrer (2002) and
   Wolvin (2005). In his successful 1964 New York State Senate run, Robert F. Kennedy
   also had to address charges of carpetbagging: no listening tour involved.
2 The upstate/downstate boundaries are wildly contested: this is an approximation.

Chapter 4

1 Many former staffers have shared stories about Clinton checking in on their personal
   lives at crucial moments (for example: https://twitter.com/emmyruiz/status/1053
   396573844054018). More broadly, former colleagues rave about her extraordinary
   ability to listen (https://www.vox.com/a/hillary-clinton-interview/the-gap-listener-
   leadership-quality).

Chapter 6

1 https://www.wcwonline.org/pdf/previews/preview_18sc.pdf
2 https://www.guernicamag.com/rebecca-solnit-men-explain-things-to-me/
3 With thanks to my former student K. H. for helping me come up with the term
   "Theory Bros."

Chapter 7

1 https://news.gallup.com/poll/190343/trump-clinton-supporters-lead-enthusiasm.
   aspx
2 https://qz.com/624346/america-loves-women-like-hillary-clinton-as-long-as-
   theyre-not-asking-for-a-promotion/
3 http://bluenationreview.com/hillary-supporters-have-the-most-enthusiasm

Chapter 13

1   After the march, participants were asked to form a "huddle" with friends and neighbors to begin taking sustained political action. Such actions, combined with the timely publication of the online "Indivisible Guide" to political organizing, should probably be credited with sparking the organized anti-Trump #Resistance.

2   Fisher (2018).

3   VanSickle-Ward and Merolla (2016).

4   Clinton (2008).

5   I was given access to make posts to five secret Facebook groups in the San Diego area. As part of a larger project, I have conducted semi-structured interviews with forty women and two men who consider themselves members of the #resistance whose lives have changed because of the 2016 election.

6   See, for example, the large number of women running for office, often defeating Bernie-backed candidates in primaries (Weigel 2018).

7   All voted. Only one said that she had voted for Jill Stein, and she now argues that she was duped by Russian propaganda. None voted for Trump.

Chapter 14

1   See Appendix Table 1.

Preface

1   https://www.usatoday.com/story/news/politics/elections/2016/03/09/clinton-sanders-democratic-debate-miami/81554434/

Chapter 16

1   Another way to counter these stereotypes is to take more hawkish stands that may counter stereotypes of women and Democrats as being weak on national security. Clinton has also followed this strategy. Given space constraints, we do not discuss this strategy in depth.

2   https://nyti.ms/1WH99LV

3 In fact, during the 2016 election, a number of national security elites on the right were supportive of Clinton over Trump. https://www.politico.com/story/2016/07/national-security-clinton-trump-225137

Chapter 18

1 https://www.youtube.com/watch?v=4ZNWYqDU948
2 https://www.youtube.com/watch?v=TyXGiHbWa6s
3 https://www.youtube.com/watch?v=f-Viu9agKuk
4 https://www.youtube.com/watch?v=U8IUUBF_E2A
5 https://www.youtube.com/watch?v=pnXiy4D_I8g https://www.washingtonpost.com/lifestyle/style/makes-going-to-work-look-easy-how-being-a-full-time-mom-prepared-nancy-pelosi-for-this-moment/2019/02/12/416cd85e-28bc-11e9-984d-9b8fba003e81_story.html?utm_term=.77c4ca92a31a
6 https://www.nytimes.com/2014/09/07/upshot/a-child-helps-your-career-if-youre-a-man.html?_r=0
7 https://www.cnn.com/2019/02/15/politics/lucy-mcbath-house-gun-legislation-cnntv/index.html
8 https://www.washingtonpost.com/lifestyle/style/makes-going-to-work-look-easy-how-being-a-full-time-mom-prepared-nancy-pelosi-for-this-moment/2019/02/12/416cd85e-28bc-11e9-984d-9b8fba003e81_story.html?utm_term=.77c4ca92a31a
9 https://apnews.com/dc67b4f47c8941bfbb0287ced06dc731
10 https://twitter.com/SenGillibrand/status/1097308079627161601

Chapter 19

1 Pantoja, Ramírez and Segura (2001).
2 https://www.washingtonpost.com/news/monkey-cage/wp/2016/12/02/donald-trump-did-not-win-34-of-latino-vote-in-texas-he-won-much-less/?utm_term=.b2cfc4f36465

Chapter 20

1 https://www.pewresearch.org/fact-tank/2016/02/03/2016-electorate-will-be-the-most-diverse-in-u-s-history/

2 https://www.pewresearch.org/fact-tank/2016/11/29/hillary-clinton-wins-latino-vot e-but-falls-below-2012-support-for-obama/

3 http://presidentialgenderwatch.org/mixed-outcomes-latinas-election-2016/#mo re-11184

4 https://www.latinodecisions.com/blog/latino-electorate-on-track-for-historic-tur nout-in-2016/

5 https://www.washingtonpost.com/news/monkey-cage/wp/2016/11/11/in-recor d-numbers-latinos-voted-overwhelmingly-against-trump-we-did-the-research/?u tm_term=.cd28b5d7896f

6 http://presidentialgenderwatch.org/mixed-outcomes-latinas-election-2016/#mo re-11184

7 https://www.cnn.com/election/2016/results/president

8 http://presidentialgenderwatch.org/mixed-outcomes-latinas-election-2016/#mo re-11184

9 http://presidentialgenderwatch.org/mixed-outcomes-latinas-election-2016/#mo re-11184

10 https://medium.com/@kelly.dittmar/no-women-didnt-abandon-clinton-nor-did-sh e-fail-to-win-their-support-77d41e631fbd

11 http://www.latinodecisions.com/files/8614/7866/3919/National_2016__Xtabs.pdf

12 https://asianamericandecisions.com/wp-content/uploads/2016/11/2016-Asian-Am erican-Election-Eve-Poll-Infographic.pdf

13 http://presidentialgenderwatch.org/racial-gender-reminders-campaign-appeals/ #more-10720

14 http://presidentialgenderwatch.org/mixed-outcomes-latinas-election-2016/#mo re-11184

15 http://presidentialgenderwatch.org/racial-gender-reminders-campaign-appeals/ #more-10720

16 http://presidentialgenderwatch.org/racial-gender-reminders-campaign-appeals/ #more-10720

17 http://presidentialgenderwatch.org/calling-attention-women-color/#more-9943

Chapter 24

1 Even after the so-called historic number of women running for Congress in the United States in 2018, less than 24 percent of Members of Congress are women.

2 Candidates for federal office are required to report any campaign contribution over $200 (although most campaigns report smaller donations as well) to the Federal Elections Commission, an agency created in the post-Watergate era in an attempt

to increase transparency in campaign finance in the United States. Federal Elections Commission data is available publicly at www.fec.gov.

Preface

1   http://time.com/3920332/transcript-full-text-hillary-clinton-campaign-launch/
2   https://www.nytimes.com/2017/06/02/upshot/how-to-raise-a-feminist-son.html

Chapter 25

1   https://www.washingtonpost.com/video/politics/hillary-clintons-emotional-concession-speech-in-three-minutes/2016/11/09/2723ceae-a69f-11e6-ba46-53db57f0e351_video.html?utm_term=.65becbbaacdb
2   https://www.washingtonpost.com/news/monkey-cage/wp/2016/07/28/here-are-3-ways-that-hillary-clintons-nomination-changes-things-for-women-in-politics/?utm_term=.04db232dddb5
3   https://twitter.com/hillaryclinton/status/740349871073398785
4   http://www.nytimes.com/2016/07/27/us/politics/dnc-speakers-sanders-clinton.html
5   https://www.washingtonpost.com/news/the-fix/wp/2016/07/28/here-is-hillary-clintons-presidential-nomination-acceptance-speech/?utm_term=.8775b4f16ffc
6   https://www.washingtonpost.com/politics/trumps-womans-card-comment-escalates-gender-wars-of-2016-campaign/2016/04/27/fbe4c67a-0c2b-11e6-8ab8-9ad050f76d7d_story.html?utm_term=.cbe0c96a8725
7   http://www.huffingtonpost.com/entry/deplorable-anti-clinton-merch-at-trump-rallies_us_572836e1e4b016f378936c22
8   https://www.usatoday.com/story/opinion/voices/2016/11/10/trump-election-white-women-sexism-racism/93611984/

Chapter 27

1   The specific question asked was: "What kind of job has the President been doing?" Thus, Donald Trump was not mentioned in this question. Yet, because this question follows one asking the children to name who the current president is, we presume that they were evaluating Trump's job performance and not that of a prior president.
2   Of the remaining 10 percent of drawings, either the image was not of a political leader or the gender of the leader was impossible to determine.

Chapter 29

1 This research was conducted as a part of the 2016 Cooperative Congressional Election Study (Ansolabehere and Schaffner 2016).

Chapter 31

1 The list was compiled by Stephen Lucas and Martin Medhurt, who surveyed of 137 leading scholars of American public address.
2 https://www.nytimes.com/1995/09/06/world/hillary-clinton-in-china-details-abuse-of-women.html
3 See Angela Davis (1983), Beth Richie (1996, 2000) and Kimberlé Crenshaw (1991).

Chapter 32

1 Placing the human rights of women and girls as central to achieving broader American foreign policy objectives is what Hudson and Leidl (2016) argue constitutes the Hillary Doctrine, Clinton's effect on American foreign policy.
2 www.hillaryclinton.com, accessed 20 November 2018.

Chapter 33

1 https://www.forbes.com/sites/tanyatarr/2018/11/07/how-the-2018-midterm-elections-could-help-women-and-boost-equal-pay-laws/#a14b910e04c0; https://www.brennancenter.org/blog/voting-problems-2018
2 https://www.congress.gov/bill/109th-congress/senate-bill/450
3 https://www.c-span.org/video/?326400-1/hillary-clinton-remarks-voting-rights
4 https://www.oyez.org/cases/2012/12-96
5 https://paq.spaef.org/article/1570/Disenfranchisement-Historical-Underpinnings-and-Contemporary-Manifestations
6 http://www.powertothepolls.com/about.html
7 https://www.cnn.com/election/2016/results/exit-polls
8 https://thehill.com/blogs/congress-blog/politics/415018-how-do-we-stop-trump-vote-like-black-women
9 http://cawp.rutgers.edu/potential-candidate-summary-2018

Chapter 34

1 https://www.cnn.com/2017/03/30/politics/joe-biden-donald-trump-hillary-clinton/index.html

2 https://www.theatlantic.com/business/archive/2016/12/hillary-clinton-working-class/509477/

3 https://www.vox.com/policy-and-politics/2016/12/16/13972394/most-common-words-hillary-clinton-speech

4 https://www.cnn.com/election/2016/results/exit-polls

5 https://www.washingtonpost.com/news/the-fix/wp/2016/12/02/in-nearly-every-swing-state-voters-preferred-hillary-clinton-on-the-economy/?utm_term=.0209ed4991be

6 https://www.mediamatters.org/blog/2016/11/02/how-media-s-email-obsession-obliterated-clinton-policy-coverage/214242

7 http://time.com/4364631/hillary-clinton-planned-parenthood-speech-transcript/

8 https://www.glamour.com/story/hillary-clinton-equal-pay

9 http://money.com/money/4422872/clinton-child-care-plan/

10 https://www.washingtonpost.com/news/wonk/wp/2015/07/13/why-hillary-clinton-made-gender-such-a-big-deal-in-her-major-economic-speech/?utm_term=.cbd9e31516f3

11 presidentialgenderwatch.org/mainstreaming-gender-in-political-campaigns-clintons-case-study/

12 https://www.americanrhetoric.com/speeches/hillaryclintonbeijingspeech.htm

13 https://twitter.com/voxdotcom/status/1037459109254234112

14 https://www.theatlantic.com/ideas/archive/2018/09/american-democracy-is-in-crisis/570394/

15 https://blogs.wsj.com/economics/2016/08/25/what-former-white-house-economists-say-about-donald-trump-and-hillary-clinton/
https://www.nytimes.com/2016/10/19/us/politics/70-nobel-laureates-endorse-hillary-clinton.html

16 https://www.theatlantic.com/politics/archive/2016/10/male-trump-voters-masculinity/503741/

17 https://www.npr.org/2018/05/10/610099506/fec-says-that-candidates-can-use-campaign-funds-for-child-care

18 https://www.politico.com/story/2018/11/26/congress-new-members-women-1014696

19 https://www.forbes.com/sites/tanyatarr/2018/11/07/how-the-2018-midterm-elections-could-help-women-and-boost-equal-pay-laws/#544ce3a4e04c

Chapter 35

1 https://www.vox.com/policy-and-politics/2016/10/19/13340828/hillary-clinton-debate-trump-won

2 https://www.newsweek.com/fact-check-trump-debate-win-hillary-1447108

3 Note, this section originally appeared in Gender Dynamics in the Final Presidential Debate: "Hot Takes from the Experts, Presidential Gender Watch," Oct 20, 2016. http://presidentialgenderwatch.org/gender-dynamics-final-presidential-debate/

4 http://time.com/4364631/hillary-clinton-planned-parenthood-speech-transcript/

5 The Hyde Amendment blocks federal funding for abortion. Clinton was the first major-party presidential president to call for its repeal.

6 https://www.vox.com/a/hillary-clinton-interview/the-gap-listener-leadership-quality

7 https://www.vox.com/2019/11/21/20975322/gender-equity-paid-leave-wage-gap-abortion-rights-kamala-harris

Conclusion

1 https://twitter.com/hillaryclinton/status/1080941776377180160?lang=en

2 https://twitter.com/ilhanmn/status/1080974474395164672?lang=en

3 https://www.theatlantic.com/politics/archive/2019/03/2020-candidates-president-guide/582598/. https://www.salon.com/2019/01/10/the-more-women-the-better-kamala-harris-and-elizabeth-warren-are-in-whos-next/

4 https://thehill.com/homenews/media/366618-vanity-fair-faces-twitter-backlash-over-hillary-clinton-video

Index

activism
    adolescent girls political
        activism 119–21
    black political activism 62–5
    Clinton's role in 3–4, 43–6
adolescent girls, political activism
    of 119–21
Affordable Care Act 156, 163
Afghan women 151–2
Afghan Women and Children Relief Act
    (2001) 150
African Americans 18, 37, 56, 89–90,
    146, 155–6
Albright, Madeleine 14, 122
Alexander, Michelle 62–3
American feminism 151–2
American foreign policies, Clinton's
    impact on 138, 141, 175 n.1
    Benghazi attacks 141, 143–4
    gender dynamics 151
    global gender effects 149–52
    multilateralism 141–4
    pivot to Asia 141–3
    women representation in 149–52
American National Election Study
    (ANES) 100
Angevine, Sarah 138
Anthony, Susan B. 56–7
anti-immigration initiative 93
Arena Summit 105
Asian Americans 97, 155
Ayala, Hala 106

Bejarano, Christina 73
benevolent sexism 101
Benghazi attacks 141, 143–4
birth control policy 162–3
black Americans 62–5
    criminal justice 64–5
    racial justice 64–5
Black Campaign School 105

Black Lives Matter movement 39, 62–5
'Black Manifesto' 18
black political activism 62–5
Bland, Sandra 89–90
Blandin, Neisha 39
Bonneau, Chris 110
Bos, Angela 81, 116
Brown-Hinds, Paulette 38
Bush, George W. 151
Bush, Laura 151

campaigns, Clinton's 3–5, 11, 20–2, 34,
    38, 47–9, 70–5, 77, 86–8, 92–8,
    119–21, 131–4, 162–5
Campbell, D. E. 116
candidacies, women 86–8, 116
Cargile, Ivy 139
Carson, Jenn 38
Cassino, Dan 160
Chamberlain, Libby 50–1
Chavez, Cesar 43
children
    Clinton's impact on 116–17, 125–7
    political leaders and 116–17
Children's Health Insurance Program
    (CHIP) 19
China's global economic
    integration 141–3
Chozick, Amy 57
Chudy, Jennifer 11
Clinton, Bill 18, 63
Clinton, Chelsea 91
Clinton, Hillary Rodham 9, 14–15,
    166–7
    accomplishments 19
    activism, role in shaping 3–4, 43–6
    American politics, impact on 76–8
    black political activism 62–5
    campaigns 3–5, 11, 20–2, 34, 38,
        47–9, 70–5, 77, 86–8, 92–8,
        119–21, 131–4, 162–5

candidacy   4, 20–1, 37–9, 42, 59, 62,
    64–5, 86–8, 115–17, 119–20,
    122, 125, 127–31, 133, 137, 160
career   3, 14–15
children, impact on   116–17, 125–7
concession speech   51, 108, 119
counterfactual effect   62–5
on economic policymaking   139,
    158–60
education   17
effect   3–5, 47–9, 104–9, 119–21,
    125–30
electoral impact of   71–5
enthusiasm   40–2
experience   76–8
fatherhood, impact on   131–4
favorability ratings   41
foreign policy approach   138, 141–7,
    149–52
gender equality and   9–10, 101, 117,
    123–4, 132, 159
health care policy, approach to   163
and Latina, 2016 campaign   96–8
Latino politics, impact on   92–5
legacy   2, 43–5, 127, 138–9, 167
loss in election   33, 56–7, 59–61,
    119–21
marriage   18
media portrayals   77–8
moms, impact on   128–30
motherhood   73, 89–91
national security experience   81–4
policymaking experience   5, 137–9,
    141–7, 149–52, 158–60, 162–5
politics, influence on   43–6
presidential elections   2–5, 37–9
public discourse   2–3
race-related issues, relationships
    with   64–5
racial justice, stances on   39, 62–5
recognition   24–6
as role model   10, 42, 74, 81, 116–17,
    138, 169 n.2
Senate campaign (1999–2000)   20–2
silence, ways to   1–2
social justice   44
speech   145
supporters   59–61
voters of   37–8, 40–1, 92–8

women's ambitions and   3, 9–10,
    13–16, 21, 71, 74–5, 110–12,
    119–21
on women voting rights   154–6
Cohen, Rabbi Jaclyn   11
Collaborative Multiracial Post-Election
    Survey (CMPS)   100
Collective PAC   105
concession speech, Clinton's   51, 108,
    119
Count Every Vote Act   154
criminal justice   64–5

Davis, Denise   74, 107–9
Davis, Jordan   90
de la Garza, Rodolfo   93
democracy, voting rights in   154–6
Democratic National Convention
    (2016)   89–91
Democratic Party   60, 63–5, 99–100
Devil is in the Details, The   164
Dittmar, Kelly   72–3, 159
Dole, Elizabeth   122
Dominguez, Casey B. K.   38–9
Duckworth, Tammy   50

economic inequality   159
economic policymaking, Clinton's impact
    on   139, 158–60
Elder, L.   90
Emerge   104–6
EMILY   105
emotions   93
enthusiasm, Clinton's
    gap   40–2
    indicators of   41–2

failure, impossibility of   56–7
faith   27–30
fatherhood, Clinton's impact on   131–4
favorability ratings   41
Federal Elections Commission   173 n.2
Feeley, Kathleen   11
feminism   13–14, 27–30, 151–2
Feminist Majority Foundation
    (FMF)   151
First Ask   105
'first daughter effect'   131–4
FMF; *see* Feminist Majority Foundation

foreign policies, American   138, 141,
  175 n.1
  Benghazi attacks   141, 143–4
  gender dynamics   151
  global gender effects   149–52
  multilateralism   141–4
  pivot to Asia   141–3
  women representation in   149–52
Foy, Jennifer Carroll   106
Frasure, Lorrie   74
Frymer, P.   63
Fulton, Sybrina   90

Gabbard, Tulsi   167
gender
  economic policy   159–60
  as electoral asset   86–8
  equality   9–10, 101, 117, 123–4, 132,
    159
  in foreign policy   138, 141–4
  global effects   149–52
  inequality   13–15, 86–8, 132
  stereotypes   72
  in strategic decision-making   86–7
gender gap
  in American presidential politics   97,
    100–2
  in elected officials   110
Gholar, A'shanti F.   74
Gillibrand, Kirsten   91, 167
Ginsberg, Ruth Bader   49
'Glass tumblers'   38, 53–5
Global Alliance for Clean Cookstoves   19
global gender effects   149–52
globalization, China's   141–3
Goodman, Amy   38, 47
Goodwin, Doris Kearns   57
Green, S.   90
Greenlee, Jill S.   73, 89–90, 116–17
Guzman, Elizabeth   106

Harris, Kamala   165, 167
Hayden, Tom   38, 47
health care policy, Clinton's approach
    to   163
Higher Heights   105
Hill, Anita   18, 163
Hillary Doctrine   150
Hispanics   92–4

Hogue, Illyse   160
Holman, Mirya R.   72, 116
homophobia   104
hostile sexism   101
Howell, Mary   57
Hsueh, Roselyn   138
Huerta, Dolores   38, 43–6

identity politics   96
Immigration and Naturalization Service
    (INS)   93
inspiration/inspiring activist   2–3, 10–11,
    15, 18, 21–2, 24–5, 33, 37–8,
    40–2
In the Running (Mandel)   87

Jordan, Barbara   155
Jordan, June   12

Kanthak, Kristin   74–5
Karpowitz, Christopher   41
Klein, Ezra   163
Klobuchar, Amy   167

Landler, Mark   83
Latina/o community   73–4, 105
  in Arizona   93, 95
  in California   93–4
  and Clinton's 2016 campaign   96–8
  mobilization   73–4, 94–8
  politics, Clinton's impact on   92–5
  voters   73–4, 92–8, 155
  voting behavior in 2016   95
Latino Decisions, polling firm   94–5
Lay, Celeste   116
LGBTQ   25, 49, 146
LGBTQIA   52
Lozano, Dc   38

McBath, Lucy   90–1
Machado, Alicia   97–8
Mandel, Ruth   87
mansplaining   31
Martin, Trayvon   90
Maxwell, Zerlina   37
media, in 2016 presidential election
    53–4
Mendelberg, Tali   41
Merolla, Jennifer L.   37–8, 72

Mexican American voters   92–3
Michelson, Melissa   117
moms, Clinton's impact on   128–30
Montoya, Celeste   138–9
motherhood   73
   advocacy and   89
   Clinton's   73, 89–91
   Democratic National Convention
      (2016) and   89–91
   in politics   89–91
   trust and   89
   vision of   27–30
'Mothers of the Movement, The'   89–90
Murch, Donna   64
Murray, Patty   90
Muslims   52

National Domestic Workers
      Alliance   167
national security, women on   81–4
New York   20–2, 77
Nteta, Tatishe   117
Nunnally, Shayla   39

Obama, Barack   96, 123
Obama, Michelle   50, 89
Omar, Ilhan   166
Osborn, Torie   38
Oxley, Zoe   116

Palin, Sarah   90
Pantoja, Adrian   73, 93
Pantsuit Nation, private Facebook
      group   38, 41, 50–2, 59
Pantsuit Nation Inland Empire   50–2
Pedraza, Francisco   95
Pelosi, Nancy   91
Penn, Mark   86
people of color   18, 31–3, 41–2, 52, 63,
      167
Personal Responsibility and Work
      Opportunity Reconciliation Act
      (1996)   63
Piscopo, Jennifer   10
'pivot to Asia'   138, 141–4
Planned Parenthood Action Fund   163
political engagement
   of women   9–10, 14–15, 71–8, 125–7
   young girls, Clinton's impact on   125–7

Praeli, Lorella   74, 94, 97
Prop. 187   93

race gap, in American politics   99–102
racial justice   39, 62–5
racial polarization   101–2
racism   18, 29, 49, 61, 99, 102, 104, 147,
      155
Ramírez, R.   93
Reed-Veal, Geneva   89–90
Renteria, Amanda   73–4, 94
representation, women   10, 13–14,
      149–52
reproductive justice   139, 158–9
Republican Party   48, 63, 65, 95, 100
#Resistance   38–9, 59–61
resistance movement   38–9, 59–61
Rhodes, Jesse H.   117
Rice, Condoleezza   83
Richards, Ann   122
Ride, Sally   122
Roem, Danica   106
role models, women   112, 116–17; *see
      also* Clinton, Hillary Rodham
Roosevelt model   76
Run for Something   105
Run to Win Program   105

Sanders, Bernie   40–1, 50, 60, 64–5
Sarathy, Brinda   11–12
Schneider, M. C.   81
Segura, G.   93
Senate campaign (1999–2000)   20–2
sexism   14, 44, 48, 61, 72, 87, 101–2, 104,
      129, 155
   benevolent   101
   hostile   101
Sharrow, Libby   117
Shelby County v Holder (2013)   155
Sherr, Lynn   56
Shook, Teresa   51
Sickle, Debra Van   10–11
Sister District Project   105
Skulley, Carrie   72
social justice   44
social role theory   81–2
Steinem, Gloria   43
Stephens, Emma   139
Stevens, Christopher   143

Taliban, women treatment in   151
terrorism   81–4
'Theory Bros'   12, 31–2
TPP; *see* Trans-Pacific Partnership
Tran, Kathy   106
Trans-Pacific Partnership (TPP)   142–3
Trump, Donald   3–4, 14, 40, 44, 50–3,
        56, 59–61, 65, 73–5, 77, 83, 92,
        94–5, 97–102, 108, 112, 116,
        120, 128–30, 142–3, 147, 158,
        162, 166
Tunis, Cortney   51

United Farm Workers (UFW) union   43
Universal Child Care   165

VanSickle-Ward, Rachel   37–8, 73, 139
Villaraigosa, Antonio   48
violence, against women   139, 145–7
Violence against Women's Act   146
Violent Control and Law Enforcement Act
        (1994)   63
Viva Kennedy Clubs   92–3
voting rights, women   154–6
Voting Rights Act (1965)   155

Wallsten, Kevin   162
Warren, Elizabeth   164–5, 167
Wellesley   10, 13–15, 25
Wells, Ida B   50
What Happened, Clinton   115
white womanhood   99–100
    political behavior   101
    vs. women of color   101
Wilson, Pete   92–3
Wolbrecht, C.   116
women   31–3, 41–2, 52, 63, 167
    Afghan   151–2
    African American   155–6
    ambitions   3, 9–10, 13–16, 21, 71,
        74–5, 110–12
    American foreign policies,
        representation in   149–52
    Asian Americans   97, 155
    candidacies   86–8, 116
    Clinton effects on   104–6, 119–21
    economic policies for   158–60

as fighter   31–3
issues   162–5
knowledge   162–3
leadership of   150
Members of Congress   173 n.1
national awakening   57
on national security   81–4
political ambition   3, 15, 71, 74–5,
        110–12
political engagement of   9–10, 14–15,
        71–8
in power position   72
representation in Latin America   10,
        13–14
reproductive rights   44
rights, in United States   38, 43–5
role models   112, 116–17
security   150
silence, ways to   1–2
social justice   44
Taliban's treatment of   151
violence against   139, 145–7
vote, importance of   74
voting rights   154–6
women of color   32, 41, 74, 97, 99–102,
        139, 147, 154–6
Women's March   51, 57, 59, 155
'women's rights are human rights'   14,
        138, 145–7, 149
Wood, Abby K.   116
Woodard, Lynette   122
working-class voters   158

xenophobia   61, 104
Xi Jinping   143

Yancey, Daunasia   63–4
young girls/women
    Clinton's campaign and   119–21,
        131–4
    political engagement, Clinton's impact
        on   125–7

Zechmeister, Elizabeth J.   72
Zero HRC Core & Cardio Life/Body
        Fitness Program   55

www.ingramcontent.com/pod-product-compliance
Ingram Content Group UK Ltd.
Pitfield, Milton Keynes, MK11 3LW, UK
UKHW020701280225
455688UK00004B/202